The Powells of Nanteos

For Thomas Lloyd

The Powells of Nanteos

GERALD MORGAN

y lolfa

First impression: 2025

Cover design: Y Lolfa
Cover images: William Edward Powell (1788–1854), left;
Edward Athelstan Powell (1879–1930), right;
both images National Library of Wales

ISBN: 978 1 80099 691 5

Published and printed in Wales
on paper from well-maintained forests by
Y Lolfa Cyf., Talybont, Ceredigion SY24 5HE
website www.ylolfa.com
e-mail ylolfa@ylolfa.com
tel 01970 832 304

Preface

THE FIRST REAL effort to tell the Nanteos story was the 2001 volume of essays which I edited, *Nanteos: a Welsh House and its Families* (Gwasg Gomer, Llandysul), more than half of it written by specialists on the house and landscape, the estate, and on the Nanteos Cup. The present book is not a re-run of that volume; it concentrates on the families of Nanteos, not because they contain any individuals of major historical interest, but because in so many ways they are typical of their class, and because they left a rich paper trail behind them. However, one squire of Nanteos was sufficiently untypical of his family and class to deserve his own chapter.

I am of course indebted to the work of the other contributors to that pioneer volume: Dr Richard Moore-Colyer, Dr A.J. Parkinson, Dr Caroline Palmer and Dr Juliet Wood, and I am grateful to Mr Michael Freeman, Mr Thomas Lloyd, Mrs Llinos Dafis, Mr Bill Hines, formerly of the staff of the University of Wales Aberystwyth Hugh Owen Library, Dr Helen Palmer of the Ceredigion Archive Service, to the staff of the National Library of Wales and of the Royal Commission on Ancient and Historic Monuments in Wales, to Dr Harry Heuser, Dr Neil Holland and other members of the staff of the Aberystwyth University Fine Arts department, and to staff at Nanteos, all of whom have borne my enquiries with kindness and help. I owe much to the friendly help and researches of Ms Janet Joel. Many thanks to the staff of Y Lolfa for their excellent work. Finally, my gratitude to my wife Enid is deep; she has lived patiently with my Nanteos and other projects for many years.

Contents

1

Introducing Nanteos

NANTEOS IS A name of poetic and historical power in Ceredigion to this day. It also conjures up other names: the name of the Powell family who owned it for two hundred and fifty years, and the name of the Holy Grail. Yet not one of these associations is quite what it seems. Nanteos is not the original name of the mansion; the Powells were not the original family who founded the estate, while the Holy Grail is a mythical vessel whose legend was invented in medieval France. Moreover, although the Nanteos estate once contained some thirty thousand acres of land, as well as lead mines which operated for at least three centuries, its wealth was not all that it seemed – for much of its later history the estate was deep in debt. Most illusory of all are the ghosts supposed to haunt Nanteos, whose numbers seem to increase with the passage of the years.

Nanteos mansion is one of the more attractive of its kind in Wales, a Georgian house set in a glorious suntrap against a background of trees. It has survived a number of crises to look much better today than it did forty years ago, when it seemed to face certain ruin and oblivion. The Powells themselves are a classic example of the rise and fall of a prominent gentry family, several of whom are of real interest, men who sometimes dreamed ambitious dreams beyond their reach – beyond their abilities and their resources.

Let's go back to the name – Nanteos. In modern Welsh it means 'stream of the nightingale', and one might suppose it to be the stream across which the mansion looks southward. Yet the stream's name has always been the Paith. That word has several meanings in Welsh, of which the most applicable are either 'open country' or 'prospect', both of which fit the scenery through which the little river flows. But Nanteos is a name seemingly invented about 1600: the original name of the house which stood on this site was Neuadd Lawdden. Neuadd means a hall, while Llawdden was an ancestral figure in this part of Wales. The medieval Welsh poet Deio ab Ieuan Du speaks of the local gentry as 'the tribe of Llawdden'. The name survives locally in the nearby place-name Rhoslawdden. Having said so much, there's no denying that Nanteos is indeed an attractive name, even though the *eos* referred to may mean simply 'songbird' rather than 'nightingale', which since records began has only been known in south-east Wales.

So much for the name of Nanteos: what of the Powells? They certainly had an estate of their own from at least the latter decade of the sixteenth century, and they acquired the Nanteos estate early in the eighteenth century by intermarrying with the previous family, the Joneses, whose story we shall also follow in some detail in the next chapter, followed by the Powell story in subsequent chapters.

Despite the vicissitudes which the place has suffered in the past, Nanteos has bewitched the families who have owned it, the men, women and children who have lived or worked here, and even people who have simply been guests in the present hotel. I first visited it in 1964, when it was still a family home and had never been on sale. It was open to the public, if I remember rightly, once or twice a week in the summer. It had a properly lived-in, slightly shabby feel and a smell of recent tobacco smoke, while the carpets sometimes showed obvious traces of the family's Pekinese dogs, not fully housetrained.

By that time the portraits on show were of third-rate quality, and there was not much fine furniture. But there was a small but good array of family silver on display on a sideboard in the drawing-room, including two sauce-boats of Cardiganshire silver which I coveted keenly, to no avail of course. We were shown what we were told was the Nanteos Cup, but which may have been a replica, though I suspect not. I regret that I have no memory of the library: perhaps it wasn't open, but it wasn't sold until later in the Sixties. Two Welsh-language books once in the collection came into my possession decades later: a copy of *Cannwyll y Cymry* with the signature of the owner, the Rev. Dr William Powell (1705–80), and a Welsh Bible with the bookplate of his great-grandson W.T.R. Powell (1815–18). The former may well have spoken Welsh as surely as English, the latter almost certainly not.

In 1964 there were, even in England let alone Wales, far fewer country mansions open to the public than there are now. The ones which were already open were 'great' houses belonging to major aristocratic families. Nanteos was unusual in being much smaller, a gentry house, without the Old Masters and classical sculptures which decorated the walls of Leviathan mansions like Petworth or Chatsworth. The embryo heritage movement had by 1964 left no stamp on Nanteos. It wasn't a place whose main purpose was to be on show: it was a home. The Mirilees family living there had inherited the house and the rump of the estate from its previous owner, Mrs Margaret Powell, widow of the last of the Powells. Their only child Billy, sole heir to Nanteos, had been killed in action in November 1918, a few days before the declaration of the Armistice.

But before introducing the families of Nanteos, we need to reach Nanteos itself. Finding the mansion today remains a great pleasure, despite the occasional pothole. We take the main road, the B4340, eastwards from Aberystwyth towards Pontrhydfendigaid. This road begins at the east end of the suburb of Penparcau, marked by a large Celtic cross commemorating Billy Powell, erected by the estate's tenants. It bends into the valley of the little river Paith, less significant than the neighbouring and grander Rheidol and Ystwyth valleys on either side.

After less than a mile on the main road we bear left along a single-lane road, with many trees on either side. There are two other houses set back from this drive: on the right is Glanpaith, a good house of 1839, while further along to the left is the more recent Rhydyfirian, once home to Dr Phil Williams, an outstanding physicist and Welsh political thinker. The last building before reaching the park is the white Italianate Nanteos lodge, designed by R.K. Penson in 1857.

On either side of the road, just before the lodge, are gates to nature reserves administered by the Wildlife Trust of South and West Wales. On the hilly side to the north is Old Warren Hill, on the south side is Penglanowen. Old Warren Hill is crowned by a large Iron Age hill-fort on a steep-sided promontory, now mostly covered by trees, especially oak and hazel. The eight-hectare area is much used by badgers. The five-hectare Penglanowen reserve, by contrast, covers the south side of the river Paith.

Here there are more ash trees, and unfortunate intrusions of rhododendron *ponticum*, which so loves the Welsh climate, but is inimical to all native wildlife. Otters, though rarely seen, frequent the river. This is a good place for birds, including pied flycatchers in summer, woodcock in winter and great-spotted woodpeckers in most seasons. Both reserves give fine displays of bluebells in late spring and there are some impressive beech trees. In the Penglanowen reserve is the largest tree of its kind in the county of Ceredigion, a magnificent *wellingtonia*. There are other fine trees to be found here and there: silver fir, cedar of Lebanon, ginkgo, Monterey cypress, beech, Norway spruce, Lombardy poplar and Portuguese laurel.

Past the lodge, our road becomes the Nanteos private driveway, rising gently past a small lake covered with water lilies during the summer; it needs dredging every few years. The lake is artificial, but is virtually two centuries old and has naturalised well. An unhurried but watchful heron may stand tall and motionless on the bank, fishing skilfully for whatever may be had. To the left rises a steep bank of trees, but to the right the Paith valley is at its broadest, and largely treeless. Here the house comes into view, facing splendidly southward across the valley, and behind it still the high tree-covered bank.

The original design of 1739 by an unknown architect would have seemed to us box-like, but it has acquired additions since then, and has grown into the landscape. At first view one should enjoy the classic Palladian design, its windows diminishing in size from floor to floor. The stonework was originally covered with stucco, mostly removed; the walls themselves are of the local Aberystwyth grits, dark but attractive when offset by the windows and other features. It is more fully described in chapter 9.

The iron railings running across the land in front of the house now divide the mansion's remaining property from the original demesne land which reached down to the Paith and up the slope beyond. All this is now farmland independent of the mansion, but it still shows evidence of its earlier use as open parkland. Originally the little river Paith must have meandered on its way down the broad valley, with many small hedged fields as shown in the earliest picture of the house (1809) known to me. But the enclosures were being swept away at the end of the eighteenth century, replaced by a broad swathe of grass with small tree plantations, and a now-ruined eyecatcher building on the opposite slope. To the right on the rise is a large woodland with conifers, Llechwedd Dyrys (tangled slope), a site which played an important part in Nanteos history. The thirty thousand acres which once powered the Nanteos estate have shrunk to the mansion and its immediate surroundings.

Straightening the course of the Paith may have made the view rather less visually attractive, but it kept the land drier for riding, walking and nineteenth-century cricket. As one walks eastward away from the car park, a stream from the high bank beyond the house, partially piped for its course past the walled garden, re-emerges to scurry away to join the Paith. At the south-west corner of the walled garden is a single brick chamber where male members of the family could relieve themselves into the stream below without having to return to the house. Just before us, crowned by a small holly tree, is the pets' cemetery, a collection of twenty-two slate gravestones commemorating hunting dogs much treasured by members of the Powell family. It has been moved a little way from its original site. Beyond this is a rather disorganised maze of stones.

The walled garden, largely enclosed by red-orange brick, with some later repairs obvious, seems enormous. The impression of size is emphasised by today's great spread of grass, with brushwood and scruff further off, and by the collapse of the two building complexes which once provided hothouse accommodation, and what may have been a gardener's cottage. This garden alone must have employed much labour to cultivate the whole area. It could certainly have provided enough fruit and vegetables to meet the household's needs, and according to tradition surplus produce would be sold at Aberystwyth market. To see what it must once have looked like, one should visit the restored gardens at Llanerchaeron.

Between the walled garden and the mansion the land begins to rise quite steeply, surmounted near the house itself by a low building known as the dairy: above it looms the coachhouse complex. This is fronted eastward by a considerable neoclassical screen, with a central arch and columns. To either side, but separated from the arch by low walls, are the gable ends of the stable ranges inside the court. These are ornamented with classical pilasters and pediments. The original effect was enhanced by stone statues above the main arch – two eagles and a horse, illegally sold when the house first changed hands. It is extraordinary to reflect that this whole effect was created when the estate was heavily mortgaged. Inside the arch, one treads on a splendid courtyard surfaced with cobbles which must surely have been carted from Tan-y-bwlch beach.

At the time of writing there are two pairs of stable units on facing sides of the courtyard. The two to the south have been restored. The western side, not normally open, has some stalls which still have horses' names above them. Turning back from the courtyard and going left up the hill, we are faced with a steep track leading to a walk through the Nanteos woodland, professionally managed for the Nanteos owner. To the right, looking east, is Woodlands House, beyond which is the old home farm and its complex, unimaginatively known simply as The Buildings. One can turn left behind the stable-coachhouse block past some portacabin accommodation to see the old dovecote, supported by scaffolding which prevented collapse when the ivy was removed. This once supplied fresh winter meat in the form of pigeon squabs.

2

The Jones Family of Nanteos

In 1592, Jane, daughter and sole heiress of Richard ap Morris ap Jenkin of Neuadd Lawdden (Nanteos), married John ap Edward ap Hugh ap Ieuan Goch. This was just at the time when ambitious Welshmen were adopting the English style of surnaming. So the children of John ap Edward's marriage would be given the surname Jones, meaning John's (son).

We know that Richard's father Morris ap Jenkin owned not only Neuadd Lawdden but a number of other farm holdings. This is clear from his will of 1565 in the Nanteos archive at the National Library of Wales. We might assume that Richard had simply inherited them from his father, but the 1565 will shows that his elder brother Owen inherited most of the estate, so Richard must have taken it over after Owen's death without a child, and Richard himself had only one child, the heiress Jane.

To marry an heiress was a good way to acquire land, because although she retained certain rights, her husband became the effective owner-manager of her estate during his lifetime. Other ways of gaining land were inheritance, purchase, lending money on mortgage or by enclosure, either legally or by simple encroachment – i.e. theft. Ownership of sufficient land led a man to the status of 'gentleman', and often to the holding of office as a Justice of the Peace. This ancient English office was only adopted in Wales after the Acts of Union of 1535–42/43. This position gave access not only to the administration of local justice, but the control of such machinery as there was of local government.

So in 1592 Jane, sole heiress to Neuadd Lawdden, married John ap Edward ap Hugh ab Ieuan Goch – at least, that's how his name appears in the documents. He would have pronounced it Siôn ab Edwart ap Huw ab Ifan; naming the four generations was an assertion of his ancient Welsh legal status as a freeman, a member of an extended family with landholding rights. Those rights no longer existed under English law, but a man's genealogy could still help to maintain a man's social status.

John ap Edward, himself already a landowner, was a fortunate man, because by marrying Jane – Siân in Welsh – he became the *de facto* owner of the Neuadd Lawdden estate 'in right of his wife'. He was Cardiganshire-born and bred: two distant ancestors in the fifteenth century had held minor office in the district under the Crown, which had ruled the area since 1277, while another owned hill farmland near Cwmystwyth, some fifteen miles inland. When John ap Edward died in 1600, his probate inventory shows him to have been a substantial farmer, owning fourteen oxen, sixty-five other cattle and a hundred and sixty sheep.

We can guess that Jane was younger than her husband: being an heiress she was probably married to him in her teens, and when John died in 1600 he had been concerned that she might be pregnant. So in his will he left the putative child £30 if a boy, £20 if a girl. He made proper provision for Jane and for dowries for their unmarried daughters. He left £5 to his illegitimate son John, three farms to his young son Richard, and the rest to his elder son and heir, Edward John ap Edward. The three farms were probably ones John had owned before his marriage; regrettably, they're not named. His numerous sheep, horses and cattle were valued at £150 at his death. Incidentally, he had arranged a good marriage for his daughter Elizabeth with 'the boy next door', David Philip Powell of Llechwedd Dyrys, of whom more in the next chapter. David was one of the witnesses of his will.

John's son and heir Edward was a wealthy landowner after his father's death. He is known in the records as Edward Jones, having adopted the English form of surname in preference to the Welsh patronymic system by simply adopting his father's baptismal name John with a possessive 's as its suffix. This was a simple way of improving his social status. Edward had made a good marriage with Margaret Lewis, daughter of the squire of a south Cardiganshire estate, Abernant Bychan. She bore Edward one daughter, Elizabeth, and a quiverful of sons: John, Thomas, Richard, George, William and James. No rentals survive to tell us how prosperous or extensive the Nanteos estate was, but Edward Jones's will of 1635 tells us a good deal about his wealth. Incidentally it tells us that for a while the family preferred the spelling *Johnes* for Jones, but this didn't last.

Edward certainly believed in the value of education. His eldest son John had been to school in Gloucester and went on to Oxford. Edward's will of 1635 laid down that John, as heir, should permit his mother Margaret to occupy all his lands for seven years while she remained a widow and did not remarry. She was to pay John £50 a year, with £12 towards his maintenance in the Inns of Court and £60 towards a Chamber and buying of books. John was clearly a law student in London; a legal training was invaluable for the owner of an estate, which continued to be managed by Margaret Jones.

John's brothers were also well treated. Thomas Jones was to be given £30 a year for seven years 'towards his maintenance in the universitie untill he become master of Arts', and then a hundred pounds 'towards his preferment' in the Church. The university was Oxford, where Thomas became a scholar of the law, publishing several Latin books on the subject; he was one of the first published Cardiganshire authors. His brother Richard, though not sent to university, was reasonably provided for. He was to be 'maintaiened at schoole with meate drinke cloathes and lodgeing' until he was sixteen, and then given a hundred pounds to place him as an apprentice. George, James and William Jones were all also to stay at school until sixteen and then become apprentices. Elizabeth was to have a dowry of two hundred pounds. No more is known of James, William and Elizabeth, but both Richard and George did better than their father had expected. They married the heiresses of two small estates, Llanina (New Quay) and Rhoscellan (in the Clarach district) respectively, which enabled them to maintain gentry status.

Edward Jones's will is valuable not only for demonstrating his wealth and his care for his family: it sets out clearly a man's duties to his family. His widow must be provided for. Unmarried daughters must be given dowries. The eldest son must inherit the estate and be responsible for the family, including his mother 'while she remains a widow and unmarried'. Thomas Jones was clearly destined to be a scholar from the start. Other sons at that time might become apprentices, thus developing social mobility, both upward and downward. Later, apprenticeships for younger sons came to be replaced by careers in the Army, Navy or the Church, thus tending to retain junior branches of families within the gentry sphere.

Edward's eldest son and heir, John Jones, ought in 1635 to have been able to look forward to a good life, but he would already have been aware of the growing political tension in the kingdom; Charles I had suspended parliament and was governing by the divine right in which he believed so passionately. In April 1642 John Jones married a Hampshire co-heiress, Mary Cornelius, thus acquiring part of a Hampshire estate, which in normal circumstances would have been a prestigious move. Their marriage agreement survives, naming twelve farms in Llanbadarn Fawr and Llanbadarn-y-Creuddyn (the latter a civil division of the former) as Mary's portion. This would only be part, perhaps a third, of the lands of Nanteos, giving us an elementary idea of the size of the estate. If the Nanteos estate at the time owned – at a guess – forty farms, with an additional share of an English estate, then John Jones was doing very well indeed. However, he had to confront two obstacles beyond his control. The first was the outbreak of civil war soon after his wedding to Mary Cornelius.

So when in 1642 King Charles I's standard was raised in Nottingham in defiance of Parliament, the great majority of Welsh gentlemen supported the monarch's cause. John Jones took a regiment of local men with him to join the royal army, as his memorial in Llanbadarn Fawr church proudly boasts. But this tablet doesn't mention that by 1645 John Jones, now styled Colonel Jones, would bring his men back to Aberystwyth to help the parliamentary army capture the town's castle, defended by royalists. This turning of his coat didn't protect him from parliamentary wrath for having supported the king in the first place, but he finally re-established himself at Nanteos, though he may have been punished with the loss of his wife's lands in Hampshire, which he seems never to have recovered.

An anonymous writer of the early 1660s gives a series of cruel pen-portraits of leading Cardiganshire gentry of the time. John Jones's apparent change of sides to attack Aberystwyth castle with the parliamentary army is attributed to 'a personal injury offered him', even though he was a convinced monarchist. We are told that he suffered severely for his loyalty, but that he was 'a man of mean parts, only wise in that he is partly sensible of the meanness of them'.

By 1663 John Jones had been named as a Justice of the Peace for Cardiganshire, thus gaining an important role in local government. For his own benefit he turned to developing Cardiganshire's only pre-industrial industry – metal mining. He had acquired a lease from the Crown through the Company of Mine Adventurers for mining in Cwmystwyth, though most of the land there was claimed by the Vaughans of Trawsgoed and the Herberts of Hafod Uchtryd. Lead and a little copper had already been mined in Cwmystwyth for centuries; John Leland on his travels in the 1530s tells of lead-mining at Craig-y-mwyn,

Cwmystwyth, and we know of it from other early leases, though (since the ore contained little or no silver) it did not draw the same attention as the spectacular exploitation early in the seventeenth century by Sir Hugh Myddleton of mines at Cwmerfin, Darren, and other places north of the Rheidol valley.

In 1663 John Jones struck an agreement with one Cornelius le Brun – by then a Londoner but originally from Cologne – for seven years for the exploitation of lead ore. The agreement was extended in the following year for twenty years, with Cornelius lending John Jones a thousand pounds to be repaid over twelve years. He would exploit the mine at Cragge Mine (Craig-y-mwyn), paying four pounds fifteen shillings in royalties per ton of ore. The mine lay on the north side of Cwmystwyth 'between two brooks'. In return John Jones promised to 'keep the miners in subjection' by all legal means. The ore was to be taken to any port in Cardiganshire or Meirionydd, and sold to a London merchant. That is the earliest information we have about the connection between Nanteos and the county's lead mines. Unfortunately the next half-century of lead-mining in Cardiganshire is a blank.

In their agreement John Jones describes himself as 'esquire', a step above le Brun's style of 'gentleman'. But clearly Cornelius le Brun was a man of some consequence, able to lend a thousand pounds to his business partner. Moreover he had soon taken his seat at the family table. John Jones had no male heir, and the estate would have to be divided between his four daughters. Anne was the eldest, and Cornelius le Brun married her. We don't know when, but it may well have been at this time (1664). Two years later John Jones died, so Cornelius became owner of

Nanteos in right of his wife. Unfortunately, we don't know how much land remained in her share of the inheritance. The three other co-heiresses all married Cardiganshire gentry, but again we don't know how much land each took to her husband. However, one of the three women's families ran out either of heirs or money, so Anne le Brun's grandson Thomas Powell was able to buy back 'the third part of the Nanteos estate' with his wife's dowry.

At his death in 1666, the list of John Jones's property made for probate is more diverse than those of his father and grandfather. He owned fewer cattle and sheep, but much more corn had been harvested than previously, which may be explained by the time of his death in the farming year. He owned a good deal of silver plate, an amply furnished kitchen, surveying implements, swords and rapiers, and playing tables – was he a card-player? He was clearly living in the style of a gentleman; he even owned books, though they are not listed separately. The inventory also names a few of the rooms in the Nanteos house: the hall, the chamber above the hall, the little chamber, the parlour. Was this house the predecessor of the present mansion? Apparently it was stuffed with furniture and the chambers with beds and bedclothing. The kitchen, apart from wooden plates, had 'brasse and iron potts & pothookes, a tin dripping-pan, a chafing dish, iron firedogs, bellows, tongs, frying shovels, spits, trivets, brandirons, bakestones & frying pans'. For the period, life at Nanteos was comfortable – far more so than the homes of the estate's tenants and labourers.

Forty-two years went by before John Jones's daughter Anne, already afflicted by her husband Cornelius's death, commissioned a memorial to her father John in 1708, still visible on the east wall of Llanbadarn Fawr church, where the family worshipped. Clearly muddled in her dating, she describes him as having died at the age of thirty-two, in which case he would have married and raised his regiment at the age of eight! He is also said to have been true 'to the Church in time of persecution [and] to the King in time of Rebellion, when for doing good, he suffered much evil', understandably forgetting his help in the token siege of Aberystwyth castle. Furthermore, '[he] in the midst of much business and tedious Trouble was a great example of Learning Himself, and a Furtherer of it to others'.

Like his father-in-law, Cornelius le Brun in his turn was disappointed of a son, having an only daughter, Avarina, born in 1675. This unusual first name took root among local families, and survives in Ceredigion to the present day. We know little of Cornelius's career, though he lived a long life before dying in 1703. Meanwhile, the future of the Nanteos estate hung, not for the first time, on Avarina's choice of husband, a choice which by the custom of the age would largely depend on her parents, but required her consent.

For a second time that choice led to a marriage with 'the boy next door' at an unknown date before 1700. 'Next door' was Llechwedd Dyrys, a mansion with estate facing Nanteos across the river Paith. As we have already seen, Avarina's great-great-aunt Elizabeth Jones had married David Powell of Llechwedd Dyrys half a century earlier. Now the Nanteos heiress would marry William Powell, David and Elizabeth's great-grandson and therefore her third cousin. So now we must ask: who were the Powells, the family which would henceforth unite the Nanteos and Llechwedd Dyrys estates?

Appendix: The 1564 Will of Moris ap Jenkin

Morris ap Jenkin of Llanbadarn Fawr was grandfather to Jane ferch Howell. His will, proved in 1565, may be of interest to local historians. Morris had four sons and two daughters. He named the eldest, Owen ap Moris, as his executor and heir, but it is clear that by 1600 Owen was dead, and that Moris's farms passed to his second son, Richard ap Moris. One of his sisters was named Jane; clearly he used the same name to christen his daughter and heiress. Neuadd Lawdden (the original house later renamed Nanteos) is not named in 1565, but that proves nothing.

3

Introducing the Powells

When Philip ap Hywel died in 1589 he was one of the richest cattle-owners in Cardiganshire. His family home was high in the Cambrian hills north of Devil's Bridge, either on the site of the present Tŷ Mawr or on a neighbouring property; a 1765 map of Tŷ Mawr survives in the Nanteos archive. Philip was buried in the little church of Ysbyty Cynfyn, a chapel of ease of Llanbadarn Fawr parish. His will, written on a substantial sheet of vellum, is to be seen in the Nanteos archive in the National Library. He left to his daughter Ellen twenty-six cattle, forty sheep and a grey mare, to form a rich marriage dowry when the time came. To one of his younger sons, Thomas, he left eleven properties which had been mortgaged to him, as well as a goodly share of livestock, together with an obligation to pay his brother, David, the sum of £40. The rest of Philip's property, unspecified, went to the eldest son and heir, Morgan, his father's executor.

As was obligatory, Morgan had to take the will to Abergwili, the bishop's administrative office, along with an inventory of his father's moveable property and his debts. In this case, Philip owed no debts, but thirty-six men owed him either money (£37.12.8d) or quantities of corn, as well as a few lambs. The inventory is short but impressive. At his death he owned one hundred and thirty-two cattle grouped by age, as well as six hundred sheep and fifteen horses. This implies the ownership of a good deal of land as well as access to the common grazing land still extensively available in the Cardiganshire hill country. Together with his household goods, which unfortunately are not itemised, the whole was valued at £207.6.8d. Although his wealth was only equalled or exceeded in the county by the owners of estates such as Strata Florida and Gogerddan, Philip only claimed the status of yeoman, a freeholder below the status of gentleman.

The Powell family claimed descent from the royal clan of Edwyn ap Gronw of Tegeingl in north-east Wales. Edwin was an eleventh-century man of mixed Welsh, English and Viking blood, whose son Dafydd Fradwr – the Traitor – sold out to the Normans. Such faraway shenanigans counted for little after so many centuries. Though Philip only claimed yeoman status, his three sons were quick to claim the status of gentlemen.

It is clear from Philip's will that matters of social status in Wales ran together with men's personal and family names. Like the Joneses of Neuadd Lawdden, Philip's sons adopted the English system of inherited surnames. Philip's will shows that the Welsh system was already breaking down during Elizabeth's reign. While Ellen the daughter is correctly named as 'Ellen ferch Philip', the sons are named as 'ap Hywel' (their grandfather), not 'ap Philip'. From this it was simply a matter of spelling for them all to be surnamed 'Powell', where the 'p' of 'ap' is absorbed by 'Hywel' and becomes Powell. Henceforth Philip's three sons were Powells.

What of Philip ap Hywel's landed property? Alas, only those properties he left to Thomas are named in the will. This was because Philip had acquired those properties by lending to their owners by mortgage. So if they could pay back the money owed, they regained the land. But land mortgaged was usually land lost, and became freehold to the next generation.

Of the three sons, Thomas the second died childless in 1604. His elder brother, Morgan, was of course the chief beneficiary. Since Morgan Powell died in 1622 without a legitimate heir, David Powell the youngest son eventually took all, though not without complications. Morgan had married Elizabeth Lloyd Pryse, one of the Pryse clan of Gogerddan, a prestigious alliance, though it produced no children. His will, on enormous vellum sheets, is exceptionally interesting. Contrary to the usual practice of not naming freehold property, the document names seventeen farms within the watershed of the river Ystwyth, four dairy-houses (*lluestai*) on the mountains, two properties in Mill Street, Aberystwyth, and several other plots in the borough. Many of the farms are still recognisable in today's landscape. They are named because, although Morgan had no legitimate child, he had two illegitimate daughters. One was fobbed off with a legacy of five pounds, but he named the other girl, Elizabeth, to be heiress to all the property.

Clearly this would never have been tolerated by David Powell, last of the three brothers and the legal heir, as Morgan well understood. So Elizabeth is to have the land 'until it is redeemed for seven hundred pounds by the right heir', i.e. David Powell. But seven hundred pounds was an enormous sum in 1622. Elizabeth, a bastard nonentity in the eyes of the law, would have been lucky to have been bought off with a dowry, and David certainly inherited the estate. But Morgan had appointed three local gentlemen as tutors (i.e. guardians) of Elizabeth, so she was probably well looked after.

Philip ap Hywel was loyal to Ysbyty Cynfyn both in life and in his grave, and Morgan also lived at 'Talcen Landwr', now Tanlan-fawr in Ysbyty Cynfyn. But either Philip or one of his sons had acquired the house of Llechwedd Dyrys in the Paith valley, facing north opposite Nanteos. It became the home of David Powell and several subsequent generations. Indeed, he only had to look north across the Paith to find a bride, Elizabeth, sister of Thomas Jones of Nanteos. She bore him at least one son, John Powell, who would eventually make a good match with Jane, another daughter of the Pryses of Gogerddan. David also had two illegitimate children: to the daughter he left farm animals, to the son he left a farm for six years, to be redeemed by the legitimate son John. We know virtually nothing else about David, so we may guess that he prudently kept his head down during the civil wars of the 1640s, presuming he lived so long. The date of his death is unknown.

Even less is known of David Powell's heir John, but his son Thomas was born in 1631, and educated at Gray's Inn. He was called to the Bar in 1660, and would for a moment play the role of non-speaking extra on the stage of national history. Although his rise in the legal profession was slow, he eventually became a judge on the north-west Wales circuit in 1685. Then, suddenly, he was made a Baron of the Exchequer with a knighthood in 1688, clearly at the choice of King James II, a decision made in desperate times. It had indeed been a dramatic time in British history. In 1685 Charles II had died, converting on his deathbed to the Catholicism he had always secretly favoured. His heir was his foolish brother James, who had already openly converted to Rome before 1685. As long as his heirs were his two Protestant daughters Mary and Anne, born to his deceased first wife, it was possible that Catholic James might have continued to rule his Protestant kingdom. But by January 1688 his second wife and queen, Mary of Modena, was known to be pregnant.

James II in his folly had dismissed Parliament for refusing to pass measures of religious tolerance. He had insisted on the drawing up of a Declaration of Indulgence, granting freedom of conscience and worship to Catholics and Nonconformists along with Anglicans. This seems perfectly reasonable by modern standards, but Catholicism was anathema both to Anglicans and Nonconformists. Following the birth of the king's son James Edward on 10 June, Church of England clergy were ordered to announce the Declaration of Indulgence from their pulpits. Seven bishops, led by William Sancroft, Archbishop of Canterbury, brought a lawsuit against the king, claiming that the Declaration was illegal. For such disobedience to the Crown they were sent by King James to the Tower of London, but at their trial for sedition before the King's Bench on 29–30 June, they were found not guilty and released, to general rejoicing.

Immediately following the verdict, James appointed Sir Thomas Powell as a judge on the King's Bench, apparently believing that he would strengthen support for the Crown. It was certainly a major promotion for an obscure judge of the Great Sessions of Wales. But when the Dutch invaded late in 1688, James fled to France, so William and Mary (James's elder Protestant daughter) were acclaimed as joint sovereigns. Powell therefore retired from London, disappointed by King James's catastrophe. He passed his last years, as his Latin memorial in Llanbadarn Fawr church insists (in translation), 'alleviating the poor and the oppressed with free counsel'.

Sir Thomas lived on until 1705. He had made another good marital alliance with Elizabeth, daughter of David Lloyd of Aberbrwynen. It was less prestigious than the alliances of his father and grandfather, but Elizabeth was heiress to her father's small estate in the neighbouring parish of Llanychaearn. Their son William's choice of wife proved even more successful; he married Avarina le Brun, the Nanteos heiress. Sir Thomas Powell showed his approval of his son's marriage by the bequest to Avarina of his best diamond ring, while his second best diamond ring went to his granddaughter Elizabeth, daughter of William and Avarina. Sir Thomas's legal career had paid off handsomely, though not as well as that of his near-contemporary Edward Vaughan, MP and London lawyer, owner of Trawsgoed, who had left two bags of gold valued at £1,100 in his study when he died in 1683. Law actually paid much better than landownership. At Sir Thomas Powell's death, his son William arranged that family burials could take place in the crypt of the chancel of Llanbadarn Fawr church by arrangement with Roger, Earl of Castlemaine, owner of the parish tithes and therefore of the chancel. The fee was ten shillings per burial.

Sir Thomas Powell apparently was not the easiest of fathers. A surviving letter from his second son Richard, written to his elder brother William, shows that, somehow, Richard had angered his father. As a result, he complained that 'the dogs have better reception than myself... I protest he is the most awkward man in the world'. Whether later reconciled or not, Richard died before his father, leaving William Powell as heir to Llechwedd Dyrys and, by marriage, to Nanteos.

*

Avarina's marriage to William Powell was more than merely a neighbourly alliance – it would, at the deaths of her father Cornelius le Brun (in 1703) and William's father Sir Thomas Powell (1705), unite the estates of Nanteos and Llechwedd Dyrys. We don't have enough details to tell which was the wealthier estate, but there's no doubt that Nanteos was the better house, and better situated in its suntrap. So William moved across the Paith to his new home, in which his wife had grown up, while Llechwedd Dyrys was left to crumble into the landscape so completely that we don't know its exact location. It must have stood somewhere within the present forestry plantation just north of the B4342 which bears its name.

The enlarged estate included much land in Ystumtuen, Cwmrheidol and the lower Rheidol valley, a number of farms in the Paith valley, Llanfihangel-y-Creuddyn and Llanychaearn. Unfortunately, no rentals survive before 1771, by which time Nanteos had taken over the Strata Florida estate. In the earliest surviving rentals the estates are listed separately as those of Aberystwyth, Nanteos, and The Abbey (i.e. Strata Florida). The Aberystwyth estate, totalling ninety-nine properties, large and small, was located in the western half of the borough within the old walls, as well as in Trefechan and the lands around Plas-crug. We don't know whether they had been originally acquired by the Powells or the Joneses – probably by both. What we do know is that William Powell went to law in 1724 to prove that he was, by historic right, Lord of the Manor. This would have given him rights over the common land round the borough. His effort failed, but would be repeated eighty years later by his great-grandson W.E. Powell, again in vain. The town itself was largely a fiefdom of the Pryses of Gogerddan.

William and Avarina Powell of Nanteos had five children, three sons and two daughters. The sons were Thomas the eldest, born in 1699, another William and John. William, born in 1705, went to Oxford and achieved some academic distinction, becoming a clergyman and a Doctor of Civil Law. John the youngest joined the Royal Africa Company, perhaps purchasing a place with his grandfather's legacy of £300. He sailed for West Africa and died there in 1737. The company, originally founded to exploit the gold of The Gambia, took also to slave and ivory trading. From 1708 its activities had been much reduced, but trading slaves continued until at least 1737.

Of the two daughters, no information seems to survive for Elizabeth, but Anne Powell married Richard Stedman of Strata Florida. Although the Stedman family had had much social and financial success in the early decades of the seventeenth century, decline and debt had set in by the time of Anne's marriage in the early eighteenth century. The union was childless, which was to prove most beneficial to Nanteos, as will become clear.

Young Thomas Powell's lack of attention to the opposite

sex troubled his father, but a surviving letter of 1721 by William senior shows his delight when Thomas at last showed an interest in a young London woman, Mary Frederick. This enthusiasm is easy to understand: Mary was the granddaughter of a wealthy London merchant, Sir Thomas Frederick, who had been Lord Mayor of London in 1661. William wrote to Mary's widowed mother in the most polished manner, begging to be permitted to bring son Thomas to call. As a result of the subsequent marriage William, already land-rich, was now cash-wealthy as well. Mary was able to borrow £2,700 to buy back on her husband's behalf a share of the Nanteos estate from descendants of one of the daughters of Edward Jones who had died in 1635.

Thomas Powell's childless marriage to Mary is something of a riddle. Portraits of her and her sisters do not flatter them; so it's easy to believe that the match was a matter of the bride's money rather than any beauty. There was certainly plenty of cash, used in 1739 to begin the rebuilding of Nanteos mansion in the Palladian style. Mary made her will in 1745, a rare event indeed for a married woman, but her family had made sure that her money was her own. Although she refers conventionally to her 'beloved husband', and paid for the return of part of the estate, there is surely irony in the words, 'I bequeath to him all interest of money he ought to have paid me upon the mortgage if any is due and £200 and the diamond ring he gave me, it's a single stone and his own enameled picture set in gold, and all my goods at Nanteos except those mentioned hereafter'. In fact she had a great deal of her furniture at Nanteos brought back to London as bequests to other members of her family, including 'my

Book Case that stood in my Bedchamber at Nanteos and all the books that Mr Powell has of mine in a Wainscott box of which he has the Key'.

So Mary Frederick died childless in 1745, possessed of £500 East India stock, nine houses and five messuages of land in the City of London, as well as her own house in New Ormond Street. Her executors were to divide £800 in cash between her family and her servants in London and in Wales, including one 'who was my Cook in Wales' and another who was 'my servant in several Illnesses that I had in Wales'. All her London furniture went to her brother Diggle Frederick, save for two mahogany pieces for her husband Thomas. She wanted all her books at Nanteos to be returned to her, as well as an extensive collection of china. One has the impression of a rather distant relationship between wife and husband, despite a portrait of the couple playing a duet together.

As for Thomas Powell himself, we have the occasional snippet of information about his character. In 1732, at a performance in Drury Lane, discontented audience members began to riot, but Powell calmed the protesters by persuading the manager to give them their money back. He would already have been known in London circles, having appeared in parliament once he had money to support his political ambitions. His limited achievements there are described in chapter 6. He was involved in the lead-mining industry; he had inherited the Cwmystwyth rights which came to him from the Powell-le Brun marriage. This was one of the most profitable of the county's many mines. During much of the nineteenth century it was still yielding Nanteos royalties of £200 per annum, while another five Nanteos mines were yielding less than £100 between them.

Powell went to great trouble to claim the Bwlch-gwyn mine in Ystumtuen. The Crown authorities insisted it was on their land, but Powell bribed with pensions three old men to say that it belonged to Nanteos. The case continued for some time, and eventually Thomas Powell won.

In 1744 Thomas Powell's brother-in-law, Richard Stedman of Strata Florida, died childless. Early in the seventeenth century the Stedmans had promised to become one of Cardiganshire's premier families, owning the Abbey demesne and much land besides, holding the office of High Sheriff once, and marrying into the major county families. But their star had faded while their debts increased. There were collateral Stedman heirs surviving, but the Stedman estate had declined in status and Richard owed Thomas Powell money. The latter therefore found himself able to take over the whole estate *force majeure*, including its lead mines.

Thomas's widowed sister Anne found herself wooed and won by the notorious baronet Sir Herbert Lloyd of Peterwell. He had found the serious Anne attractive thanks to his transient fit of Methodistical piety, but the attraction soon faded. Anne soon separated from him to live a quiet life on her own, perhaps remaining in the Strata Florida house. There is a memorial to her in Strata Florida church. Apart from that possibility, we don't know who moved into the Strata Florida mansion until the first surviving Abbey rental of 1771, when the tenant was Nathaniel Williams, esquire, son of William Williams of Pant-y-siryf, Tregaron, known as 'king of the mountains' on account of his vast flocks of sheep.

In 1752, only eight years after Thomas Powell had brought off his coup at Strata Florida, thus considerably enlarging the Nanteos estate, he died suddenly of a heart attack on a London street, and like Richard Stedman, he was childless. The heir was his younger brother, the Rev. Dr William Powell. Within three years he had paid off the mortgages and other debts on the Strata Florida estate. As a clergyman he was ineligible to stand for parliament, and although a Tory by family tradition, he achieved a successful relationship with his Whig neighbour Wilmot Vaughan of Trawsgoed, third Viscount Lisburne, and supported his political ambitions. It is thanks to Wilmot that we know that 'my best friend' William Powell sent his son, another Thomas born in 1745, to Westminster School, where Wilmot visited him more than once, and sent favourable reports to his father.

Both William Powell and Wilmot Vaughan had considerable interests in the lead-mining industry, which was flourishing in north Cardiganshire despite the near-impossibility of smelting the ore locally, as well as many geological difficulties. There were there too many shortages of water above ground to drive waterwheels consistently, while underground too much water often flooded the workings. It may well have been William's involvement in lead-mining which motivated him to become in 1754 a founding member of the Society for Encouragement of Arts, Manufactures and Commerce, now the Royal Society of Arts.

The two Nanteos and Trawsgoed landlords, along with the Pryses of Gogerddan, had trouble with Lewis Morris, superintendant of the Crown mining interest in Cardiganshire. Morris was a highly gifted but choleric character who was doubtless serving his own interest as well as that of the Crown. As Morris rightly complained in 1745, 'Mr [Thomas] Powell and his solicitor live on the spot, and are all guilty of encroaching [on Crown land] and are men of Fortune here'. At one point in 1753 William Powell and his allies organised the arrest of Morris at pistol point, and he was taken to Cardigan gaol. Morris was soon released, but was deprived of his Crown office. After that he had to content himself with bilingual rants in letters to his brothers in which he described Powell as 'a blue son of Satan and a thorough rogue', and in untranslateable Welsh as a 'ffagl o wellt pys cric crac yn chwilboeth' (feebly rendered by me as 'a bonfire of crackling burnt pea-straw'). He could only offer a coarse comment on the death in childbirth of Powell's wife Elizabeth in 1757.

Lewis Morris's brother Richard, a confirmed Londoner, gives us sardonic evidence of William Powell's life in the capital. Richard wrote to Lewis describing how in 1760 Powell had joined the Society of Cymmrodorion:

> amusing to see the Powell put five golden guineas in the poor box when he had the honour of being sworn a Cymrodor in our last meeting! Your brother Richard is great chums with Powell! What would you give for such an honour?

and again:

> Powell told me in the meeting room that he had never, and would never, raise his tenants' rent by one penny. What a good heart! He put another gold guinea in the poor box the last time he was with us.

All this must have stung Lewis Morris to the quick.

In 1759 William Powell leased his mining rights to an

outside prospector, Chauncey Townsend, and from then on the Nanteos mines (at least eight in number) were exploited by a series of companies who paid royalties on their product. Although profits could fluctuate quite violently from year to year, in the best times Nanteos could draw more than two thousand pounds a year in royalties, leaving relations with the exploiters to their agents.

By his own evidence at least, William Powell was a good landlord. He certainly took an interest in his estate as well as the lead mines. In 1764 he commissioned a mapping survey, farm by farm, of the estate, as well as a map of the Nanteos demesne. These, including the demesne map, can be seen in the National Library of Wales and give us evidence of the patterning of the landscape and the use of the land. Powell was also involved in the affairs of Aberystwyth borough. In 1755, like some of the other county gentry, he had himself sworn a burgess, with the right to vote in general elections (though none was held during his adult life or for long afterwards) and in town affairs. At a meeting of the Court Leet in 1770, along with five other gentlemen, he undertook responsibility for rebuilding the town's Guildhall. His son Thomas was sworn in in 1766, aged twenty-one. William Powell died in 1780, leaving to his heir an estate which was so extensive and various in its nature as to demand great skill in its management.

Apart from numerous properties in Aberystwyth and north Cardiganshire, even as far as Lampeter, at one time or another there were a few holdings in Pembrokeshire and in Carmarthen town, an estate in Montgomeryshire (Llanbrynmair) and a poorly documented estate in Merionethshire – not to mention the six vast Breconshire sheepwalks which Margaret Stedman had long ago inherited from her father. This mini-empire constantly shifted shape thanks to acquisitions and sales. Its income was not proportionate to its spread: in 1785 the total income from rents, lead-mining royalties, sale of animals and of oak bark for tanning was £2,935.10.3d. In fact the demands made on this income by mortgage interest, repairs and capital expenditure, family pensions and allowances, kept the estate's agents constantly pressing for economies.

William and Elizabeth Powell had secured the future of the family line before 1757 by producing Thomas, and one daughter, Corbetta Williama, who married William Lewes of Llanaeron (now Llanerchaeron). This Thomas Powell, already thirty-five when he inherited, was a man with a vision well beyond his means. He had his portrait done in pastel by Thomas Lawrence, and in 1793 commissioned John Davenport to produce an ambitious plan for reshaping the Nanteos landscape. It would have involved creating a large lake with two islands, as well as a tower, a temple, a rotunda and other buildings. To achieve this, the six nearest tenanted farms would have been incorporated into the scheme. There was to be an eastern entrance to the demesne to match the existing western one, both with gated lodges, the whole to be made accessible by no less than twelve miles of new carriage drive. Given the limited resources of the estate, the plan was idiotically ambitious.

Thomas Powell had already begun to make such a transformation seem possible, thanks to his influence in the local turnpike trust. At one time the main road from Aberystwyth to Tregaron had passed up the Paith valley within close view of the Nanteos mansion. But the gentry class in general had become increasingly unwilling to endure public voyeurism. At Nanteos the turnpike trust provided for the closure of the route in front of the mansion and its replacement by the present B4340, which has a fine view of the mansion but from a much greater distance than the original road. Thomas Johnes of Hafod masterminded another road all the way from Aberystwyth through Moriah, Capel Seion and Devil's Bridge (now the A4120) and on through Cwmystwyth to Rhaeadr (B4574), while closing the original roadway in front of Hafod.

Davenport's extraordinary plan for Nanteos remained largely a dream. Thomas also had visions of reaching the House of Commons, but he repudiated his father's alliance with Wilmot Vaughan of Trawsgoed, and suffered as a result. His hopes of influencing the 1783 election were destroyed by Vaughan's superior political generalship. Eventually the Nanteos estate, one of the largest in Cardiganshire, fell at Thomas Powell's death in 1797 on the shoulders of his nine-year-old son, William Edward Powell. It came with a burden of his father's debts which was never to be shaken off.

4

Interlude: Nanteos in 1793

How would the Nanteos of yesteryear strike a visitor from the 2020s? The year 1793 is not chosen at random; we are fortunate in having a detailed 'inventory of the household goods at Nanteos' taken on 3 March 1793 by Thomas Robson, the newly appointed agent for the estate. It was made on the understanding that Thomas Powell, his wife Eleanor and their young family, intended to move for a while to London, which they did in 1795, at which time Robson would move into the mansion.

One of the great virtues of the list is that all the furnishings are listed room by room, with each room identified. However, it is not so easy to identify the listed rooms with those of the present mansion, which has been much altered and extended since the inventory was drawn up. The present hotel's large dining room was an extension made after 1800, probably replacing a smaller room. No wings were added to the east for many years after the list was drawn up.

Naturally enough, Robson worked from the entrance hall, which was sparsely furnished, and then 'the Dining

Parlour', which I guess was the room to the right of the entrance now subdivided and used by reception staff. The room was well furnished for its purpose, and had nine family pictures on the walls. If this guess is right, then the 'Drawing Room' may have been what is still a sitting or drawing room to the left of the entrance. The problem here is that the present room seems too small for the 'large dining table', two mahogany card tables and a bookcase, with other furniture, and eleven pictures on the walls. But where then were the Little Parlour (with two bookcases and eight pictures) and the Little Hall? Perhaps these were the two rooms to left and right of the entrance, with the Dining and Drawing Rooms contained to the left after passing through the entrance hall. At this point we should note that Robson paid attention to the coal boxes which were in almost all the larger rooms; doubtless logs were in constant use along with coal to heat the house. Coal was brought by ship to Aberystwyth from the Pembrokeshire mines for those who could afford it.

The rest of the ground floor was taken up with 'offices': the kitchen, the servants' hall, the butler's pantry, the housekeeper's room (really her office), the laundry and the still-room. Of these much the most interesting was the Servants' Hall. As well as the expected tables, chairs and benches there were twenty-four javelins, thirteen hangers (short swords), three pistols, one blunderbuss and two pictures. At that time of conflict with France, those weapons were not simply for ornament. Also intriguing are two of the objects in the butler's pantry: a backgammon table and a map of Europe, apart from the furnishings one would expect. Why would the butler need a map of Europe? Did any of the Powells make the Grand Tour?

It seems unlikely, though the lovely marble mantelpiece carving in the Music Room might be a memento of such an event, otherwise uncommemorated.

More prosaically the laundry contained the expected tubs, clothes horses and flatirons, while the still-room held – what else? – the still. The still-room is something of a riddle, since the *Shorter Oxford English Dictionary* offers several definitions. Was it a distillery for producing alcoholic spirits? Was it for the production of perfumes and cordial drinks, the original meaning? Or was it a room in which preserves, cakes, liqueurs, etc. were kept, and tea, coffee, etc. were prepared? Thackeray wrote that 'a hundred years ago, every lady in the country had her still-room'. So choose – gin or preserved fruit, or both; perfume seems less likely.

Robson then climbed the same fine staircase that we use today, but noted only the carpet, though it is difficult to believe that there were no pictures on the walls. Then we encounter another mystery. The heart of the first floor today is of course the main gallery, but Robson named 'the Best Gallery' and 'the Gallery' separately. Yet the former had only a barometer on the wall, while the latter, though on the second floor, was crowded with 'eight family pictures, thirty-seven historical pictures, fifty-nine views in Wales, twenty-four prints without frames, two long prints with frames and glasses, two prints without frames views in Wales, four pictures of "Flowers with frames and glasses", a clock, two family pictures, a bookcase.' One might have expected to see a display of pictures in the best gallery, but it is clear from the context that the 'best' gallery is on the first floor and the other on the second floor. The former is named with the main bedrooms, the latter with rooms which were quite obviously on the second floor.

The grand room off the gallery is today loved for its fine mirrors and wonderful plasterwork, and is used for weddings. For many years it has been styled 'the Music Room' or the 'Salloon', as Robson describes it. He only refers to 'two Pier Looking Glasses', suggesting that the great wall-mirrors we see now must have been added after 1793. This saloon was clearly a music room, since in 1793 it had a pianoforte. It must have been rather a crowded space, with its large and small dining tables, two card tables, two marble tables and a small writing table, not to mention a sofa and 'ten Cotton bottomed Chairs'. The three window curtains were green.

Also on the first floor were the main bedrooms: Mrs Powell's Room with dressing room, the 'Mackcaw Room', the 'Room over the Kitchen', the 'Best Room', the 'Pink Room' and a room whose name is illegible to me: is it the Fens Room, the Tens Room? It's definitely not the Men's Room, in case you are inclined to guessing; it was furnished like other good bedrooms in the house. Since the front left-hand room was still known as the Pink Room in the twentieth century, it may be supposed that the front right-hand room was Mrs Powell's. It was well-furnished, including a 'night-chair' or commode, and a bookcase. The dressing room must have been crowded, having in it a bureau, dressing table, two 'Wash Hand Stands', a desk, four mirrors, an arm chair and five other chairs, as well as a 'Dressing Stool'.

Elsewhere in the inventory one finds 'Mr Powell's Dressing Room', but did he have a separate bedroom? My understanding is that it was common at this period for the lady of the house to have her own bedroom separately from that of her husband. If this is correct, then the 'Best Room' with its extensive range of furniture was probably his. At least it was close to that of his wife, though he had to climb to the second floor to reach his dressing room.

I guess that what was recently known as the 'Yellow Room' may have been the 'Mackcaw Room', since some species of macaw have bold yellow breasts. This, like the 'Best Room' and the 'Room over the Kitchen', were all comfortably furnished. The only mysterious item of furniture, at least at first glance, is the 'biddy', one in the Pink Room and one in Mr Powell's room on the second floor. These were obviously bidets, well-known to travellers in the eighteenth century. Unlike today's bidets, they would have been portable, not plumbed in; housemaids or footmen would have brought and disposed of the water.

The second floor was reached by the 'Common Staircase', still in its place today, and was used both by family and servants. On this floor were the housekeeper's bedroom, 'the servant men's room', the gallery full of pictures described above, a 'Room over the Mackcaw', the White Room and the Check (all with matching bedstead curtains) Rooms for Master Powell and Miss Powell (i.e. William Edward and Ellen – in 1793 their younger siblings had not yet been born); both rooms were well-furnished. The last rooms on this floor were the 'Little Lodging Room', presumably for guests, and Mr Powell's Dressing Room, which had 'Thirty Pictures and a Frame', an alarm clock and mirrors, and a bidet. Upstairs again were the 'Garrets', quite well-furnished, presumably for the use of female servants.

At that point Thomas Robson seems to have come

back downstairs to deal with the remaining household offices: the kitchen, store room, cellar, brewhouse, dairy and the malt room. The kitchen contained large quantities of pewter, iron and brass plates and cutlery, tins, family table, and three brass kettles. There was also a 'hastener'. This was used when roasting a joint or bird in front of a fire: it was a reflective screen put the other side of the roast to reflect heat back. I'm not sure where the store room was, but it was a busy place, holding nine brooms, twenty-five hand brushes of different sizes, seven mops, eighteen copper stew pans and saucepans, a lot of old bottles with old wines, distilled waters and preserved gooseberries, six dozen new pewter plates, eleven new pewter dishes, ten old plates, not to mention six dozen measures of flax and hemp and one dozen of spun hemp. These last were used for making ropes and coarse fabrics.

The cellar was also a busy place, at least for the servants. It held ten stands, presumably for holding the twenty-one half-hogsheads, four hogsheads, a hamper of corks, two brandy casks, five iron hoops and four brass cocks (i.e. taps). Then somewhere outside were the brewhouse and dairy, perhaps in the building near the north-east corner of the house. The brewhouse held two coolers, four troughs, five 'vessels for working the beer in', 'seven buckets for carrying the beer into the cellar', three buckets for working the beer, two mashing forks, two hop baskets, one stand for same, an iron hook to open the furnace door with, and a malt mill. A hundredweight of malt was kept in a separate room. Nothing could better emphasise the importance of beer in a country house of the period. The dairy, too, was vital: it contained an old coffer, two brass pans, three iron pots, five milk trays, seven cheese vats, two cheese presses, one cheese tub, two churns and four milking pails.

Two questions stand out: first, where were the bathrooms and lavatories? The simple answer is that in 1793 there weren't any. A number of the bedrooms had washstands and/or bidets, the former probably of the marble-topped kind with ewer and basin, emptied and filled by the servants. For night-time use there were 'night-chairs', either commodes or close-stools, in some bedrooms, but not all. There must have been some provision downstairs, but what exactly it was is a mystery. At this period some major houses were provided with privies and running water, and one has to presume that at Nanteos there were outside privies kept clean by servants.

The second question is simpler: where was the library? The easy answer according to the inventory is that there was no library, only bookcases in a number of rooms. But the room now containing the hotel bar was definitely the library at some time, and was photographed early in the twentieth century with orderly stacked shelves full of fine bindings. In 1793 this room may have been the 'Little Parlour' with its two bookcases.

A related question derives from the survival in the Nanteos archive of the undated 'Inventory of Mr Powell's Music'. The handwriting is of the early nineteenth century, and so does not refer to George Powell (1842–82), a well-known music lover whom we shall meet in a later chapter. This inventory seems to be the earliest information we have of musical life at Nanteos, which must have been quite active.

This inventory consists of six pages listing the titles of well over a hundred works, including some by Mozart

(1756–91), Haydn (1732–1809) and Beethoven (1770–1827). There are symphonies and sonatas, but much of the music consists of songs and pieces for piano, and duets or small groups of musicians, mostly for violins and cellos. Among the lesser-known composers whose works were in the collection were F.H. Hoffmeister (1754–1812), J. Mazzinghi (1765–1844), Sir John Stevenson (1761–1833), William Shield (1748–1829), and music from the *Circassian Bride* by H.R. Bishop. There are numerous songs, a few still well-known, like 'Oh dear, what can the matter be?' and 'The Boys of Kilkenny'. Others are unknown to me, though they produce hits on-line, for example 'The Mischievous Bee', 'The Lovesick Frog' and 'The sigh of her heart was sincere'. Perhaps all these works were kept in the Saloon or Music Room, where the japanned cabinet would have served well.

A slightly later inventory of 1809, when W.E. Powell reached his majority and took formal ownership of the estate, is a valuation of the Powell silver, made by Makepeace and Harker of London. The number of items is astonishing. The list is eighty-nine lines long, many of them naming multiple items. For example, five table candlesticks are valued at £72, while several single items were rated highly, a tea urn at £67, a punchbowl at £90, and an *épergne*, a table centrepiece, with eight branches and twelve basons at £156. The total value by weight is given as £1,757.16.0. The collection continued to grow during the following hundred years, but is now all scattered, probably destined to be melted down. The sauce-boats which I so coveted (p.10) are not evident.

It may have been after the deaths of William Beaumont Powell and his wife in 1911 that a typed inventory was drawn up of all the furniture at Nanteos. The list of rooms is intriguing, especially when compared with that of 1793. The listed order of the rooms is rather confusing, since it moves erratically between the floors:

> Front Entrance Hall, Office, Morning Room, Top Floor Valet & Chauffer's room, Top Floor Butler's Room adjoining, top floor Lavatory (has a mahogany Toilet Paper Box), Top Floor Night Nursery, Top Floor Painting Room: Locked. Top Floor Japanese Bedroom, Ditto, Japanese Ante Room, ditto Mrs Edward Powell's bedroom, top floor upper gallery: numerous pictures including photographs of four Wagner operas, plus more, 2 Servants' bedrooms.
>
> First floor: Damask Room, Damask Dressing Room, lavatory adjoining. Pink Room, Pink Dressing Room, Grand Saloon, with grand piano, music stands and stools, Mrs Powell's Bedroom, with ante room, Mr Lewis's Room, Green Room.
>
> Main Corridor, including goldfish aquarium, rosewood music stand with 44 books of music, cuckoo clock, cabinet of curiosities. Mr Powell's Dressing room. Main Staircase. White Hall, Library: this included a Stuffed White Mole, one print of the acquitted Seven Bishops of 1688, one musical box with 12 records. Dining ante-room, Dining room.

There is no mention of the kitchen, cellar or billiard room.

A time traveller from today to either 1793 or 1911 would have found the house crammed full of stuff. For example, apart from all the furniture, in 1911 the entrance hall alone contained two eagles, two white pheasants, one heron, a cock and hen pheasant, an 'Old Welsh Kite', a golden pheasant, a wild duck, a trout and a lizard, two fox heads and brushes, and the following armaments: two small brass cannon, a dozen rifles with bayonets, four carbines, four horse pistols, thirteen swords in sheaths, five battle axes and one dirk. The rifles and swords are a reminder of the roles of W.E. Powell and W.T.R. Powell as Cardiganshire militia commanders.

5

Nanteos Family Life, 1797–1878

FROM THOMAS POWELL'S death in 1797 onwards the history of Nanteos and the Powell family becomes more complicated. That is mainly because the sources multiply, especially reports in Welsh newspapers, which only came into existence at the beginning of the nineteenth century, and particularly Cardiganshire local newspapers from 1840; these show an increasing interest even in the most mundane details of landowners' lives, occasionally revealing more sensational details which could not be covered up. I have preferred to deal with the family's involvement in politics in chapter 6.

As we have seen, Thomas Powell's death left his nine-year-old son William Edward as heir to the extensive Nanteos estate. This chapter will give priority to family life, but reference to the estate is necessary, since throughout the period its stability was seriously threatened by debt, rash expenditure and mismanagement. W.E. Powell's own son and heir, confusingly also christened William, with the additional names of Thomas Rowland, is best therefore known as W.T.R. Powell, and his story will end this chapter.

The boy William Edward was naturally in the care of his widowed mother, who had three younger children to manage as well; these were William's sisters Ellen and Anne and his little brother Richard. Unfortunately the widowed mother, Eleanor (née Corbet), originally of Ynysymaengwyn in Merionethshire, emerges from her late husband's shadow as a woman with no sense of the value of money. This was particularly unfortunate since in 1797 the estate's debts already ran to £12,000. This could have been easily controlled by skilful management of resources, but no-one took proper charge. Eleanor's extravagance was not tempered by any great wisdom on the part of a succession of agents and trustees supposedly responsible for oversight and financial administration. For example, in 1814 the great Welsh architect John Nash was asked to suggest improvements, producing lovely drawings which survive in the Nanteos archive, including an entrance lodge and a new facing for the mansion's western wall, but nothing was done. This was fortunate for the estate's finances, since Nash's employment was expensive.

Life in the Nanteos countryside did not appeal to Eleanor Powell; she soon established her young family in London, which added considerably to her expenditure. It was inevitable that she would eventually find herself in debtor's exile where creditors could not pursue her, first in Dublin and later in Calais. But young William Powell had to be educated, so he was sent to his father's old school, Westminster, and on to Christ Church, Oxford. He then joined the Army, an expensive profession for a would-be officer; in 1807 his commission as captain in the Royal

Horse Guards ('The Blues') cost the estate £700. Nor would his Army pay have ever met his regimental expenses as a cavalry officer in London and Bath. Indeed, Army life, even during the Napoleonic Wars, did not prevent him from spending a good deal of his time enjoying the social life in Bath. His lack of early years in Wales, and his subsequent career in London, suggest strongly that he had no knowledge of or interest in the Welsh language, unlike his grandfather, the Rev. Dr William Powell.

In 1809 William celebrated his coming-of-age at Nanteos, but was soon back in Bath, much preferring the social round in the company of a young lady to his new responsibilities for the estate, where the debts had increased to £20,000 and rising. A second effort was made about this time to justify the claim (first made in 1724) to establish the Powell right to be Lords of the Manor in Aberystwyth, but again the claim failed, though it cost the borough so much in legal expenses that they had to lease out the common land round about the town.

To add to his responsibilities, William had been appointed High Sheriff for Cardiganshire for 1810, the year in which he married Laura Phelp, the young lady who had caught his eye in Bath. She was a beauty, daughter of James Tufton Phelp of Coston House in Leicestershire, but alas for Nanteos, her gentry family was penniless. Laura's only prospect was of a £3,000 dowry when her father died, and he a man whose own estate was heavily in debt. Correspondence unearthed by Dr Caroline Palmer suggests that Laura was already pregnant before the wedding took place at St Nicholas outside Cardiff; if so, the baby must have died. Realising that Army life in The Blues was beyond his means, William took up a commission in a regiment of infantry instead, and in 1812 he was given the rank of major. This transfer was a rare example of economy on his part.

At least one historian has suggested that William Powell was interested in promoting agricultural improvement. The only evidence offered is an advertisement in the *Carmarthen Journal* in 1810 offering twenty-seven prizes for which Nanteos tenants might compete, including crops of turnips, clover seed, hedging, fencing and enclosing, and for planting apple trees. However, the remainder of his career offers no further trace of such worthwhile activities: instead there is repeated evidence of landlordly neglect, extending even to allowing the Nanteos wine-cellar to be rifled by servants, especially George White, the bibulous butler during the 1840s, to whom were attributed the words:

> Nanteos ale both strong and stale
> Keeps my nose from looking pale.

Soon after William's own wedding in 1810, new marital alliances were to cause the estate further financial embarrassment. His sister Ellen was contracted to marry Laura's penniless brother, Edward Tufton Phelp, and the two were married in 1811. Ellen was entitled to a dowry of £5,000 from the Nanteos estate, which was just as well for her husband Edward, since he had no money of his own and could expect little from his father, whose debts were double the value of his estate. Although Ellen's dowry was probably not handed over at once, it would have acted as a credit account on which the young couple might draw as needed – and it must surely have been badly needed. By this time, too, Eleanor Powell's debts had been paid off to the sum of £3,500, and a loan of £2,500 provided for her, all at the estate's expense.

Further trouble would arise with the marriage of William's younger sister Anne Corbetta to the unpleasant and abusive Roderick Richardes of the small Penglais estate at Aberystwyth, though she didn't leave him until after the birth of the last of her six children by him, and a formal separation was not arranged until 1848. In the meantime, in 1828, the youngest of the four Powell siblings, Richard, succeeded in marrying well with Harriet Wynne of Peniarth, who bore him a son, William Beauclerk Powell. Against expectations, this boy would eventually inherit Nanteos.

Army service did not help William and Laura's marriage. In 1811 he had to take his regiment for two years to Ireland, where he received ever more dolorous letters from his lonely wife, complaining that she felt neglected and couldn't pay household bills for lack of funds. Even on William's return to Britain in 1814, he was in no hurry to reach Nanteos, but once he did arrive home Laura quickly became pregnant and in 1815 gave birth in Swansea to a son and heir, William Thomas Rowland Powell. That accomplished, Powell took himself off to London. He returned briefly to father a second son, Cornelius, in 1817; the choice of name reflects some interest in family history (for Cornelius's place in the family, see the endnote to this chapter). In 1818 came what may have been the most dangerous incident in William Powell's life; when he travelled to see his mother in France, his ship was wrecked, but he escaped unscathed.

William Edward Powell's rank and status in

Cardiganshire made him a potential parliamentary candidate, and the opportunity came at a by-election in 1816. This followed the death of Thomas Johnes of Hafod Uchtryd, who had been the county's member since 1796. Pryse Pryse of Gogerddan might have claimed priority, since the Gogerddan interest dominated county politics, but Pryse's personal link to the county was rather less solid than Powell's. Pryse was the son of Edward Loveden Loveden of Buscot Park and the Gogerddan heiress Margaret Pryse. Young Pryse preferred his Welsh roots, and so had changed his surname from Loveden to Pryse, his mother's maiden name. He was willing to wait for the borough seat to become vacant at the next general election, due in 1818.

This left William Powell able to canvass vigorously for the county seat, which he gained without opposition, and held it without any formal contest for the next ten general elections. Such a void did not mean that the county's politics were totally moribund: there could be alarms and excursions, and sometimes a threat of opposition at the polls, but nothing materialised. For his and his son W.T.R. Powell's political careers, see chapter 6.

W.E. Powell, like his father and grandfather, chose to spend time in Bath and London rather than near his tenants, let alone near his wife Laura, as already noted often abandoned at Nanteos. Parliamentary time certainly had to be spent in London. Given that necessity, added to Powell's generally heartless treatment of Laura, it is hardly surprising to know, thanks to the researches of Ms Janet Joel, that he had acquired a mistress in London.

She was a Mary Gennet, and may have attained her unenviable relationship with Powell before his election to

Parliament in 1816; she regularly used his surname as her own. Between that year and 1830 she bore him four children. The first three, all boys, were baptised in 1829 under the Powell name, though their father was so negligent of this alternative family that they had to depend on Camberwell for parish relief. At one stage William was told that Mary was 'in a very woeful plight indeed'. So was his wife Laura, who clearly knew of Mary Gennet's existence before she had died in 1822, protesting to the last her loyalty in the face of her husband's cruel neglect. It was perhaps soon after 1830 that Mary and her children emigrated to New Zealand; one may imagine that Powell contributed to the cost of their passage, since their existence was clearly an embarrassment. Powell eventually remarried in 1841 with Harriet Dell (née Hutton), widow of George Ackers of Moreton Hall, Cheshire. The marriage was childless.

Although Powell was often absent from the county, he was certainly willing to see developments in Aberystwyth, of which his estate owned a considerable part, especially in the old borough town. Most of the rest belonged to Gogerddan. The medieval castle and its surrounds were Powell's: so were Laura Place (formerly Laura Gardens, named for his wife), Pier Street and Market Street. The fine Assembly Rooms were built by 1820 to provide for the wealthiest of the increasing number of holiday visitors to the town. Membership cost a guinea a week, which gave one access to English-speaking company, with card-playing facilities, newspapers and dances. From 1827 Powell or his agents were responsible for building the fine houses in Laura Place, and the smaller houses in New Street. The largest house of all, now numbers 11 and 12, was originally the Nanteos town house.

Rural distress certainly caused Powell some concern. It drove people to protest against the payment of tithe and church taxes[1], against inflation and the impositions which they suffered because of the tollgates. In 1843 and again in 1844 the Rebecca rioters of Pembrokeshire and Carmarthenshire inspired some fellow-sufferers in the Teifi valley, and as far north as Llannon, to destroy tollgates. Powell himself was a turnpike trustee as well as chairman of the county's magistrates, who were responsible for law and order. Both troops and Metropolitan policemen were sent for, involving unpopular expense to ratepayers. The government favoured the establishment of a police force, a financial responsibility which the magistrates had hoped to avoid on grounds of expense. The county's first policemen were appointed in 1844.

The economic condition of the Nanteos estate remained precarious, although occasional retrenchments, including the sale of lands Powell owned in Montgomeryshire[2], and of his Newmarket racehorses, enabled him to survive without disgrace, which could otherwise have forced him to give up his parliamentary seat. Every so often he would change his lawyers and agents, especially if they nagged him about his inefficiency. By 1823 his mortgage debt was

---

1 Tithe payments, based on the products of agriculture and fishing, were originally intended for parish churches, especially the incumbents' salaries, but for centuries north Cardiganshire's tithes were pocketed by the Chichester family of Arlington, Devon, who lived high on the hog and paid pittances to vicars and curates, and were in theory responsible for maintaining the Llanbadarn Fawr chancel. Church taxes paid for church running expenses, and were resented by Nonconformists.

2 This was sold to John Conroy, a figure notorious as the man who so abusively controlled the household of the young Princess Victoria that on her succession to the throne in 1837 while still a minor, she immediately banished him from the Court.

£58,000. His income had increased dramatically thanks to inflation to nearly £9,000 a year, which by the standards of the time was enormous wealth, but in fact most of it was already committed, and like many landed gentry, he was often strapped for cash. Nevertheless, a gentleman was expected to be generous. One such expense was the perceived need for a better church building in Aberystwyth; in 1827 Powell subscribed £250, joint top subscriber with Pryse Pryse of Gogerddan, to build the first church on the Laura Gardens site.

Despite his problems, Powell gave a good deal of attention to the Nanteos mansion, improving the frontage and providing spacious stables and coach-houses with a noble entrance. These building developments in the 1820s, 1830s and 1840s seem to have involved more effort on Powell's part than his parliamentary activity. A portrait of him in old age reflects nothing of his popularity and general bonhomie. Another portrait known to have existed shows him resplendent in military uniform as colonel of the local militia. Unfortunately, it appears to be lost: a dreadful garish copy used to be exhibited on the mansion staircase, but has mercifully disappeared. By 1854 his health had become too fragile for him to continue in parliament: he resigned his seat in February and died in April. By then his heir, W.T.R. Powell, was nearly forty.

W.T.R Powell had grown up mainly in England, where he had all his schooling, first in Totteridge, then at Westminster. But he did not follow his father to Oxford, possibly for economic reasons. Instead he joined the 37th Regiment of Foot in 1832 as an ensign and sailed for service in Jamaica, only a few months after British and local soldiers and enraged colonists had brutally put down the serious slave rebellion (the 'Baptist War') of December 1831. More rebels were executed than colonists killed in the revolt. By 1834 Powell's regimental commander had to ask W.E. Powell to pay £500 to cover his son's debts, from which time he agreed to a £500 annual allowance for his son. Powell must have left Jamaica prior to his marriage in 1839, and we know that he brought a black servant home with him, mentioned by his wife Rosa Powell in a letter of 1854 as 'Col. Powell's former Black servant'. I can find no further mention of him.

After his father's death in 1854, W.T.R. left the professional Army, and was designated colonel of the Royal Cardiganshire Militia in his father's place. As owner of Nanteos he retained much of his father's status in the county, though he was not yet an MP, nor did he ever become Lord Lieutenant of the county as his father had been. He had inherited an estate much encumbered by debt; the Abbey and Tregaron estates alone were mortgaged for £55,000.

Four serious misfortunes befell Powell. One was his disastrous relationship with his wife and children. In 1839, aged twenty-four, he had married the twenty-one-year-old Rosa Edwyna Cherry, daughter of W.G. Cherry, who had for a time been Powell's agent and friend, but after Cherry had been relieved of his responsibilities the friendship turned to enmity. This had not hindered the marriage, but when that relationship soured, Cherry was naturally on his daughter's side. She bore Powell two children, George Ernest John Powell in 1842 and a daughter, Harriet Edwyna, born in 1844. It is clear from the correspondence that Rosa Powell was willing, up to a point, to excuse her husband's vacillating and indecisive nature. She blamed the bad influence of his friends for his behaviour, but she clearly suffered greatly from his attitude, which changed through indifference to hostility.

Two hundred and fifty letters, now in the Ceredigion Record Office, deal with the breakdown of the marriage. In 1853 W.T.R. Powell was seized by the wholly unjustified suspicion that his wife was intimate with another man, a Mr Patterson. He wrote to his father-in-law, Mr Cherry, telling him of his determination to secure a formal separation from Rosa. She in her turn accused him of intimacy with Sarah Lord, the children's governess. Following numerous letters between the two parties and their lawyers, as well as with others, Rosa accepted that a formal separation was inevitable. She was in the heartbreaking position that her husband held the whip-hand, both financially (she had to accept a meagre allowance of £300 a year, though wanting more) and in his legally guaranteed control of the two children, amounting to virtual ownership.

Although Powell admitted that Rosa had to be allowed to see her children, he made it as difficult as possible until her death in 1860. Rosa had had to make repeated efforts to keep him even to his harsh promise of only three visits a year, and those only in the presence of third parties. Their son George became convinced that his father's behaviour had been responsible for the eventual deaths both of his sister Harriet in 1857 and their mother in 1860, and loathed him for it. There are small memorials to Rosa and Harriet in the Llanbadarn Fawr chancel, where the girl's name is rendered as Harriott. Neither stone mentions W.T.R. Powell either as husband or father, as would have been normal in a happier family.

The second disaster in W.T.R.'s life was illness. It seems

that about 1859, after being elected to parliament as member for the county, he began suffering from a paralytic disease which incapacitated him for the rest of his life, compelling him to use a wheelchair. This may explain why it is so difficult to find any record of his presence in the House of Commons when he became the county's MP. The third disaster again concerned marriage, this time a case of breach of promise.

A remarkable verbatim report survives in the *Aberystwyth Observer* for 18 February 1865. It sets out in full the speech of Mr Coleridge, a barrister appointed to defend Powell in the court of Queen's Bench on a charge of breach of promise, brought by Miss Margaretta Lewis, claiming £50,000 in damages. She apparently knew Powell because her sister Hannah (or Anna) was married to W.T.R.'s cousin William Beauclerk Powell, grandson of W.E. Powell and the eventual inheritor of Nanteos in 1882. The relationship must have caused all parties much embarrassment when the scandal broke, especially in Aberystwyth.

Mr Coleridge cheerfully admitted to the court that the defendant really had made a promise of marriage to Miss Lewis at a party at Nanteos in 1864, as the result of a joke about it being a leap year, when it is (or was) believed that women may propose marriage to men. Powell had subsequently given her a diamond ring worth fifty guineas. Coleridge claimed that there was no evidence of any affection between the two, and that a marriage between them would have been sexless and therefore unconsummated on account of Powell's semi-paralysed condition.

Moreover, Powell was in financial straits because 'he has habits which one of the witnesses said he had not been weaned from', whatever that may mean – heavy drinking, perhaps. Coleridge asserted that Miss Lewis was simply hoping that Powell would have to settle his estates on her. Therefore, as a mature woman who knew perfectly well that this would be a marriage in name only, she deserved only trivial damages. At the time she was twenty-six, Powell almost twice her age. Despite her hopes, Miss Lewis had to be content with the court's eventual verdict – £2,000. Even that much-reduced sum must have been an embarrassment to the strained finances of the Nanteos estate, while the newspaper reports must have caused much sniggering in London and Wales. But Miss Lewis would gain an unexpected bonus when W.T.R.'s son George died in 1882, as is explained below.

W.T.R. Powell's fourth problem, already hinted at above, was the hostility between him and his only son and heir, George, subject of the next chapter. Powell lived on for another thirteen years after the trial for breach of promise, and when not staying in the South of France he maintained the style of life expected of the squire of Nanteos. The *Aberystwyth Observer* repeatedly refers to his patronage of local events. Cricket matches were often held on the land in front of the mansion, which he enjoyed watching. The newspaper is full of references to hunting, especially hunt dinners and to the hunts themselves, usually in pursuit of foxes and otters.

The most remarkable of the Nanteos hunts was surely the stag-hunt arranged in April 1876. The species of stag is not named in the press report, though it was presumably a red deer brought from an English estate. The poor creature was released on open ground near Nanteos; it then fled hither and yon for many miles, pursued by hounds, horses and riders until it eventually leapt the Penparcau tollgate and ran down the steep hill to the Rheidol. Plagued by the hunters, it leapt into the river and was carried downstream. When it was seen to be drowning (perhaps in the harbour at high tide), one of the huntsmen leapt into the water to seize it by the neck. The account doesn't say what happened next, but one presumes it was slaughtered. Incidentally, Dr Caroline Palmer unearthed correspondence of this period in which W.T.R. Powell offered to provide a stag to Powis Castle for hunting, but how it would be obtained is a mystery; Nanteos never had a deer-park.

However, W.T.R. was not simply a Tory hunting squire. He enjoyed patronising concerts, and gave Tregaron a public library. More remarkably, as a boy he had shown interest in drawing, and in later life he created a number of scrapbooks full of his own work. Many of them are charming humorous sketches, including realistic sketches of people hunting and fantastic drawings of hundreds of tiny midges in human postures. But he does not seem to have been a pleasant man to know. To give a single example, it seems clear that when his son George was at a preparatory school near London, W.T.R. asked the school to intercept letters to the boy from his mother.

W.T.R. Powell was often abroad or in London, but there are newspaper accounts of lively occasions at Nanteos at which he presided. In August 1873, for example, there was a splendid ball, attended by two hundred and thirty named guests, with another dozen groups in attendance, so three hundred people must have sat down at tables in the Long Gallery and elsewhere. Before and after the feast there was dancing to the Leicestershire Militia Band. This kind of outward display could not conceal the estate's financial weakness; land sales had begun, and between 1868 and 1873 land was sold to the value of £82,617.

In 1867, in an extraordinary development prior to the first sale of Nanteos land, W.T.R. Powell's son George, then twenty-five years old, brought a suit in the Court of Chancery against his father and his father's cousin and agent William Phelp, to restrain them from reckless felling of trees near the mansion. The estate's chief woodman, David Edwards, had been sacked after thirty-five years' service for protesting. His affidavit not only described the follies he had been asked to commit (carried out after his dismissal), but the appalling conditions of several farms known to him, where the house had tumbled down. One tenant was living in a cowhouse, another in a barn. The felling, which included two harvests of twelve tons of oak-bark for the tanning industry, was obviously done to raise money quickly. The court apparently found in George's favour.

In May 1878 Powell died in London and the body of 'the gallant gentleman', as he was conventionally known on account of his military rank, was brought by train to Aberystwyth for burial outside the east wall of Llanbadarn Fawr church, alongside the graves of his estranged wife and his young daughter. It was a rather diminished estate than George Powell inherited.

Endnote: Cornelius Powell (1816–64)

The direct male Powell line would fail when George Powell died childless in 1882, to be succeeded by his father's cousin, William Beauclerk Powell (d. 1911). But descendants of Cornelius Powell (I), second son of W.E. Powell, flourished. He himself had been named for his ancestor Cornelius le Brun. His career is something of a mystery; his father had made him an allowance of £300 a year, but by 1859, while living at Lochaber in Scotland, he had lent his elder brother W.T.R. £1,500. How he managed this is not known. He died in 1864, having been a lieutenant in the 1st Dragoon Guards. Cornelius (I) had three sons, Cornelius (II) le Brun Powell (1851–1927), Athelstan Edward Powell and George Frederick William Powell. All these first names occur in earlier Powell generations.

Cornelius le Brun Powell had four sons, all given family first names followed by le Brun Powell. Two of this generation, Charles William and Cornelius (III), both had sons, and the latter's sons and grandsons have the le Brun Powell surname. Daughters were not named le Brun, but were given first names from earlier generations. The youngest representative of this line at present is the Rev. Edward le Brun Powell, who serves at the time of writing in the parish of Caerphilly.

Several of these Powell descendants lived at Sunny Hill, a small gentry house north of Tregaron. It had become the focus of the Sunny Hill estate, which appears to have been carved out of the extensive Nanteos estate for the use of subordinate members of the family. Thus, prior to Cornelius (II), William Edward Phelp became W.T.R. Powell's agent and lived at Sunny Hill until his death. He was the son of the 1811 marriage of William Edward Powell's sister Ellen to Edward Tufton Phelp, and therefore first cousin to W.T.R.

It would be interesting to know why none of this flourishing cadet branch of the Powell family was considered (at least as far as is known) as potential heirs to Nanteos when the line of succession died out in 1930.

Did any of them receive an offer, only to decide that the inheritance would involve too much trouble and expense? I have been unable to find out.

6

The Powells in Politics

THE KEYNOTE BY which to understand British electoral politics in the eighteenth and early nineteenth centuries is best expressed in the traditional phrase 'Old Corruption'. The whole circus is wonderfully parodied in Charles Dickens's account of the Eatanswill constituency contest in *The Pickwick Papers*. All women and most men had no direct representation. Bribery was rife, intimidation and violence not unusual. So gentry families, who held all the power in Wales as did the aristocracy and gentry in England, would collaborate to ensure the election of their own by avoiding expensive polls whenever possible. But the fact that constituencies might not have a single contest in decades didn't mean that there was no politicking – far from it. Canvassing and compromise were of the essence.

There were two parliamentary seats for Cardiganshire: the county and the boroughs. It was especially necessary to the gentry not to contest the county seat, since the many hundreds of eligible voters were too many to be bribed, even though they were only a minority of the adult male population. So it was much more convenient to agree, even with opponents, to adopt only one candidate for each seat. As for the boroughs (Cardigan, Aberystwyth, Lampeter,

Tregaron and, in theory, Adpar), the landed proprietors who 'owned' each borough could secure the appointment of burgesses, the men who supposedly tenanted a burgage plot and therefore had the right to vote in the borough elections. Whether these men actually lived in the borough hardly mattered.

So if it came to a contest for the borough between two of the leading families, they would appoint large numbers of new burgesses to the boroughs they controlled in order to swing the vote. This too was best avoided by compromise, since all the burgesses would at the least expect to 'eat and swill' at the candidates' expense. Nanteos owned a good deal of Aberystwyth land, but Gogerddan always had the controlling interest, as they did in Cardigan. Lampeter 'belonged' to the Lloyd family, while Nanteos only controlled Tregaron, which eventually lost its borough status.

A second difficulty in grasping the politics of this period is the matter of 'party'. Two political factions emerged from the hurly-burly of the so-called Glorious Revolution of 1688–89: the Tories or Court party and the Whigs or Country party. These were not parties in the modern sense, but semi-fluid interest groups without membership cards or parliamentary whips. Candidates didn't publish manifestos, only anodyne statements of support for the Church of England, the country and the Crown. Roughly speaking, the Tories saw themselves as supporters of the monarchy and its rights, and of the Church of England. Whigs sought to limit the king's power and rights and supported tolerance for Nonconformists.

Many Tories regretted the 1714 succession of George of Hanover as heir to Queen Anne, last of the Stuart dynasty.

Some at least would have welcomed a Stuart return in 1715 or 1745, had either Pretender's rebellion been successful. But Welsh Jacobites, as the Young Pretender complained in 1745, were reluctant to do more than drink his health. The only exception was David Thomas Morgan (1695–1746), originally of Glamorgan, executed for his loyalty to the Young Pretender. Welsh MPs at this time generally lacked any group coherence; only infrequently did they concern themselves with 'Welsh' matters. Nor did they aspire, with few exceptions, to do more than wield the considerable local patronage and influence which Members of Parliament had.

The hierarchy of power and influence in Cardiganshire was for centuries headed by the Pryses of Gogerddan. The Vaughans of Trawsgoed owned more land, but Gogerddan had the greater influence in who should stand, especially in the borough seat. Consequently, at least thirteen Gogerddan family members, relatives by marriage or friends sat at one time or another for one or other seat, compared with only seven Vaughan family members and three Powells of Nanteos. The surname Lloyd marks out some ten descendants of the Castell Hywel dynasty who sat for county or borough, but they had become a diffuse clan with many independent estates rather than remaining a nucleated family. Family loyalty was of the essence, overriding party interest.

Political allegiance to Tory or Whig did not prevent cooperation between families. The Tory Powells' alliance with the Whig Pryses, both originally Jacobite by inclination, was sufficiently close that when Edward Pryse of Gogerddan died childless in 1699, his will decreed that failing all surviving male Pryses, his whole estate would pass to William Powell, though matters never became so desperate. William and his father Sir Thomas were among those named guardians of the actual heir, the child Lewis Pryse, who would become known as a Jacobite.

William Powell of Nanteos was decidedly Jacobite in temper. He and Lewis Pryse of Gogerddan were reported to the government in 1710 as having gathered with other gentry in Aberystwyth to drink on their knees to the Pretender's health and return to the throne. In 1717 the county's Lord Lieutenant, the first Viscount Lisburne, described Powell and Pryse as 'the greatest incendiaries and most disaffected persons in the principality of Wales... managers of the correspondence between the malcontents in North and South Wales [whose] agents so terrified the people in general that neither the commissions issued out by me, nor even the orders of the Privy Council [could be put into execution]'. But nothing came of this self-interested rhetoric.

The first Powell to stand for parliament was Thomas, grandson of Sir Thomas Powell the judge. Following the death in December 1724 of the sitting member for the borough constituency, Stephen Parry, Powell was successful at the subsequent by-election, but in the 1727 general election he was persuaded to stand down in favour of Francis Cornwallis of Abermarlais, Carmarthenshire. Instead, Powell agreed to stand for the county constituency against John Vaughan of Trawsgoed, the scandalous second Viscount Lisburne, but his effort failed.

Thomas Powell was nothing if not persistent. In 1729 the borough MP Francis Cornwallis died, so Powell stood again at the subsequent by-election for the seat. He appointed eight hundred new burgesses for the miniscule borough of Tregaron, which he controlled, although there could never have been so many actual burgage plots, nor eight hundred male inhabitants in Tregaron itself. It was enough to carry the vote on the day, but at the subsequent appeal the House of Commons committee ruled that Tregaron was not a borough, so Powell was disqualified in favour of Richard Lloyd of Mabws. He tried yet again in 1741 for the county against the sitting member, Walter Lloyd of Peterwell. Lloyd was returned to parliament by 344 votes against 340, but Powell petitioned against the result and in 1742 was declared the victor. In 1747 he retired at the end of the parliament, having voted consistently against the government of the day, and was replaced by John Lloyd, son of Walter.

The aggrandisement of Nanteos by its union with Llechwedd Dyrys could have enabled the Powells to become consistent contenders for the county's parliamentary seats. But Thomas seems to have had his fill of politics by 1747; he died, childless, five years later. His younger brother and heir, the Rev. Dr William Powell, was disqualified from election by his priestly status. This did not prevent him from playing an active role in alliance with Trawsgoed. Dr Powell's son Thomas seems to have been more ambitious for his estate than for political advancement. So although the Powells remained influential in county political arguments and alliances, it was not until Dr William's grandson, William Edward Powell, came of age that a Powell would again sit in the Commons.

Despite W.E. Powell's debts and the precarious condition of the Nanteos estate, the young man led a charmed social life. Advancement, like popularity, came easily to him: he was appointed county High Sheriff at the age of twenty-two for the usual period of one year. In 1815 the county MP, Thomas Johnes of Hafod, died childless and bankrupt; Powell canvassed vigorously for the seat and was returned unopposed. This was apparently the result of the toss of a coin between himself and Pryse Pryse of Gogerddan.

Thus effortlessly, with little in the way of any political talent or any patronage from London, William Powell had reached the summit of Cardiganshire's political life. The only advantage denied him was promotion to a baronetage, or even a peerage, for which his applications were rejected, fortunately for the tottering finances of Nanteos. Welshmen were hardly ever granted House of Lords peerages before 1800, and rarely afterwards; it was more usual for Welsh titles like Carnarvon [*sic*] and Denbigh to be granted to Englishmen. Even the Dynevor peerage was created for an Englishman, the Earl of Talbot, to be followed by his half-Welsh daughter, wife of George Rice of Dynevor, and their descendants. The only Cardiganshire peerage, the Lisburne title of the Vaughans of Trawsgoed, was an Irish title, inferior in status to an English title and having no guaranteed seat in the House of Lords.

The following year, still in his mid-twenties, Powell was made Lord Lieutenant of the county, a life appointment; he had thus reached the pinnacle of county social and political life, with direct responsibility to the Crown. He was unfortunate in that these positions demanded considerable expenditure which he could ill afford. In 1819, for example, he could not afford to pay for the coach he had ordered in London. But he was fortunate in that this was a time when other major county families (e.g. the Vaughans of Trawsgoed and the Lloyds) were in temporary eclipse, while Pryse Pryse of Gogerddan agreed to wait until he could be elected for the borough seat at the next general election in 1818. Powell and Pryse stood in this partnership through the general elections of 1826, 1830, 1831, 1832, 1835, 1837, 1841 and 1847, thus ensuring that no voting took place for either seat. The two men were not assiduous in attending parliament, and when they did their votes frequently cancelled each other out. When Pryse died in 1849 he was succeeded unopposed by his son and heir.

W.E. Powell and Pryse Pryse had not enjoyed complete peace of mind during their political careers; numerous figures from in and beyond the county were named as possible challengers, but for decades none came forward. They had to present to the Commons their constituents' petitions, against Catholics, in favour of Reform, to oppose timber duties and to improve Aberystwyth harbour. Nonconformists (not allowed to vote, but able to petition) sought to strengthen Sunday observance.

Powell's political career, such as it was, followed Tory practice. 'Steady as she goes' for the benefit of Church and country would have served as his motto. He could see the terrible post-Waterloo poverty which afflicted Cardiganshire, where the landless could be forced to continue the squatters' traditional resort of building *tai unnos*, one-night houses on common land. This included squatting on common land over which the Powells had ownership rights.

However, Powell seems to have done little about the dire conditions of the poor, other than to present to the Commons in 1817 a county petition on 'agricultural distress'. He also opposed the tax on sea-coal, a levy which bore on the rich rather than the peat-burning country folk of his constituency and estate. Over the period up to 1832 he presented numerous other petitions from the county which reflected its increasingly Nonconformist culture: people deplored slavery, rejected any move to allow the emancipation of Roman Catholics, but favoured parliamentary reform: to the latter the Tory Powell was personally opposed.

All was not peace and quiet in Cardiganshire, much as Powell and his gentry colleagues might have wished it so. There had been food riots in Aberystwyth in 1796 and again 1816; there were enclosure riots in several parishes between 1816 and 1818. The disturbances caused by the folly of the incomer Augustus Brackenbury ('y Sais Bach', the Little Englishman) flared up in 1820 and again in 1826. Brackenbury had outraged the folk of Mynydd Bach by attempting to enclose the common land which he owned but over which cottagers had traditional rights on which they depended for economic survival. There was growing pressure for the creation of a police force, which Powell as the Crown's representative in the county tried to resist as long as he could, mainly on account of the expense that would be involved. There were disturbances in Cardigan in 1837 and again in the area in 1838; the magistrates pleaded for troops to be sent, but troops had to be billeted in the towns, which was most unpopular.

Two issues in Parliament involved some activity on Powell's part before the end of the 1820s. The government proposed to reform the Welsh system of Courts of Great Sessions to bring justice in Wales into line with English legal practice. Many Welsh Tories, including Powell, opposed the change, but it was carried through nevertheless, thus removing the last remaining distinction between Wales and England, save only the nebulous status of 'Principality' and the occasional existence of a 'Prince of Wales'.

The Reform Bill crisis of 1831–2 caused Powell something of a personal crisis. At his arrival for the Cardigan Sessions two years previously, he had been met by an enthusiastic crowd who took the horses from his carriage and drew him into town themselves. They seem to have been more concerned with preventing Catholics from having the vote, though there were virtually no Catholics in the county. Powell's principles were against reform of Parliament; he had previously voted against allowing the inhabitants of the great towns of Birmingham, Leeds and Manchester to have any representatives in Parliament, while the county of Cornwall had more than sixty MPs. However, he well understood that reform was a cause favoured by his constituents, so he compromised by keeping away from the debate, but voting for the Reform Bill in 1832 to satisfy his constituents. He may well have understood that it was not nearly so revolutionary as its enemies painted it, and his caution did not diminish his popularity in the county.

In the subsequent election of 1832/33, Powell and Pryse were both re-elected without opposition. The reform improvements, minimal as they were, counted for little, so the gentry's throttling grip on the county's electorate continued until 1841 for the boroughs and 1859 for the county. In an undated squib, Powell was abused under the title of 'Mr Poverty Placeman', a comment on the county as well as on Powell.

Local issues continued to present problems. Cardiganshire's roads, like those of the rest of south Wales, had been largely turnpiked, with gentlemen like

W.E. Powell ready to invest in the trusts, which they could then control. It became possible for them to re-route main roads away from the vicinity of gentry mansions, as was managed at Nanteos, Hafod and Trawsgoed. But the tolls became increasingly burdensome to farmers who had to buy and sell at weekly markets, and when this coincided in the 1830s with the commutation of Church tithes from crops, stock and fish to cash, survival became increasingly difficult. Added to this was Nonconformist resentment at payment of tithes, which was supposed to go to the Church, although most Cardiganshire tithes had long been impropriated by gentry families, so that they could live well by the sweat of poorer men. That of course was in addition to the separate issue of Church rates (for purchase of candles, linen, etc.), again enforceable on Nonconformists.

The effect of the Rebecca riots in Cardiganshire was limited compared with that further south. But in 1843 four toll-gates in the Teifi valley were smashed and troops dispatched as a result. This did not prevent further trouble, this time in Llan-non, and William Powell appealed successfully to the Lord Chancellor for the appointment of more local magistrates; in 1844 the county police force was finally established. By then protest was dying down, and with the effective nationalisation (anachronistic as the term is) of the Welsh turnpike roads, the rioters' work had been successfully done.

In parliament, Powell remained loyal to Conservative principles ('no change') and Tory governments. But when the Tories split in 1846 over Robert Peel's repeal of the Corn Laws, allowing cheaper imports to feed the country's bulging population, Powell deserted Sir Robert Peel's government to vote against the repeal. Late in his career Powell had hoped to gain exemption from Church rates for Nonconformists who contributed to their chapels as well as their parish churches, but had to withdraw his Bill.

William Edward Powell remained the county's MP until 1854, when he resigned, dying a few months later. This necessitated a by-election, but again Old Corruption ensured the successful nomination of Ernest Augustus Vaughan, fourth Earl of Lisburne. Like Powell and the Pryses, father and son, Lisburne was silent in the House of Commons, and gave up the seat in 1859. At last there was a contested election for the county seat.

The candidates this time were both Tories: Arthur Henry Saunders Davies of Pentre, Carmarthenshire, and William Thomas Rowland Powell of Nanteos, son and heir of W.E. Powell. Saunders Davies may well have been the better candidate, but W.T.R. Powell's influence in Tregaron and Aberystwyth ensured his victory at the polls, the first contested election for the county seat in the nineteenth century. As a Member of Parliament, Powell was even less distinguished than his father; he was in declining health and eventually confined to a wheelchair. He only voted in sixteen divisions during his whole tenure of the seat. He did not contest the election of 1865, but lived on until 1878. He was the last 'parliamentary' Powell. His obituaries did what they could to disguise the increasing hollowness of the role of the major rural landlord. Following the democratic parliamentary reforms of the 1860s and 1880s, it became impossible for anyone of Cardiganshire's gentry class to be elected to the House of Commons.

7

George Powell, the Aesthete

Nothing brightens up a family history like the presence of an eccentric, preferably one with at least something of the character of a black sheep, though George Ernest John Powell was neither blackguard nor rogue in that traditional pattern. However he certainly was 'different', vividly unlike any of his ancestors, or indeed any contemporary of his class in Wales known to me. A later generation, however, would see George's foibles extravagantly outdone by Evan Morgan, second Viscount Tredegar (1893–1949).

Born in 1842 in Cheltenham, George was the only son and heir of the irascible W.T.R. Powell and his unhappy wife Rosa. In many ways we know more about him than any previous member of the family, though he only once held public office, had no interest in politics and died when only forty years old. George Powell would grow up to publish poetry and Icelandic folk-tales, to be a competent pianist and lover of classical music, a traveller to Belgium, Iceland, Denmark, Germany, Morocco, Spain and especially France, to appear in the reminiscences of the Goncourt brothers and the memoirs and fiction

Nanteos from Llechwedd Dyrys
Private collection

Nanteos entrance hall, ?1930
National Library of Wales

Nanteos main gallery, ?1930
National Library of Wales

Nanteos Music Room, ?1930

National Library of Wales

Nanteos principal staircase

National Library of Wales

Seventeenth-century sauce-boat of Cardiganshire silver
Private collection

Nanteos mansion

The Rev. Dr William Powell, 1705–80
National Library of Wales

Ceramic jug promoting W.E. Powell

Private collection

William Edward Powell, 1788–1854

National Library of Wales

Edward Athelstan Powell,
1879–1930
National Library of Wales

Dorothy Wilding portrait of Billy Powell, 1899–1918, in Scottish military dress
National Library of Wales

W.T.R. Powell (1815–78) by William Roos

Private collection

Ink drawings by W.T.R. Powell

National Library of Wales

Strata Florida Abbey

Llanddewi-brefi

Roman Baths of Caracalla

My Dream by W.T.R. Powell

National Library of Wales

George Powell, 1842–82
National Library of Wales

George Powell in Moroccan dress
National Library of Wales

Algernon Swinburne, 1837–1909
National Library of Wales

Eirikur Magnusson,
1833–1913, Icelandic scholar
National Library of Wales

Jón Sigurdsson, 1811–79,
Icelandic patriot
National Library of Wales

The Lady of the Mountain (Fjallkonan), a symbol of Iceland, by J.B. Zwecker
University of Aberystwyth School of Art

Frontispiece to Powell, Magnusson, Jón Árnason's *Icelandic Legends*, 1866

National Library of Wales

Papal Bull

University of Aberystwyth School of Art

Clare Vaughan Morgan, by Dante Gabriel Rosetti

University of Aberystwyth School of Art

Moon and Sleep, by Simeon Solomon

University of Aberystwyth School of Art

Seraph, by Edward Burne-Jones

University of Aberystwyth School of Art

Love Dreaming, by Simeon Solomon

University of Aberystwyth School of Art

The Wounded Dove,
by Rebecca Solomon

University of Aberystwyth
School of Art

Crystal Casket from
the Powell bequest

University of Aberystwyth
School of Art

Japanese Netsuki

University of Aberystwyth School of Art

Japanese Kagamibuta-netsuke

University of Aberystwyth School of Art

Cruet, given to George Powell at his wedding

Private collection

Early 20th-century photograph of the Nanteos Cup

National Library of Wales

of Guy de Maupassant, and befriend the poet Algernon Swinburne. He was an avid collector of books, of printed and manuscript music, and of paintings, prints, drawings, sculpture, ceramics, coins, Japanese netsukes and what are called in Welsh *trugareddau* – small memorabilia of many kinds.

All that sounds interesting but harmless enough, and indeed there's little doubt that George Powell was socially popular in the London circles he favoured. Even after his father died in 1878, London remained the focus of his life, though he returned to Nanteos occasionally, and under pressure eventually accepted the annual appointment as Cardiganshire's High Sheriff. He was a generous patron of the School of Church Music, of Icelandic culture, and of Aberystwyth's newly created University College of Wales.

However, as we have already seen, George Powell's childhood was unhappy. He must have perceived the chasm growing between his parents even before his mother was forced to leave Nanteos when he was eleven and his sister nine. She was the innocent victim of the process of legal separation instigated by her husband, described in a previous chapter. W.T.R. Powell did all he could to obstruct the children's visits to their mother, and after his sister Harriet died in 1857, George (then fifteen) would forever hold his father responsible. As already mentioned, in 1867 George had even brought a case in the Court of Chancery against his father, seeking to stop him felling timber on the Nanteos estate.

George Powell was largely indifferent to the hunting, shooting and fishing pastimes beloved by his father, which his predecessors and his gentry contemporaries took for granted. Challenged by his father to go out and shoot something, so the anecdote tells us, worn smooth by much repetition, George went out and shot one of his father's prize bullocks. As well as his rejection of rural pastimes, there was indeed something different about George. After home education by a governess, he had eventually been sent on from Cheltenham Boys' School to Eton; that brutal establishment seems to have left a permanent mark on him, as will be seen.

George Powell's adolescent interest in Iceland and Icelandic culture presumably derived from the attention already being given to the island's remarkable literature by English scholars, which he must have encountered while still a schoolboy at Eton. It's true that he wasn't the first Welsh gentleman to show some interest in the subject; William Vaughan, Corsygedol (1707–75) owned a copy of Thomas Percy's *Five Pieces of Runic Poetry* (1763). But why did George choose Iceland? It's true that he had already been to Belgium for the first of his travels. Iceland may well have been associated in his mind with the general interest of the day in Arthurian and other romantic medieval legends. But the only clear evidence is that in 1860, aged eighteen, George had privately published two volumes of his juvenile poems under the pen-name Miölnir, the name of Thor's hammer in Nordic myth, printed in Aberystwyth by John Cox in 1860 and 1861. He wrote the epilogue to the first volume on 3 December 1860, and the preface to the second in February 1861, both in Brussels, so even before going to Iceland he had visited the Continent.

Clearly, therefore, George knew in his teens of Icelandic culture, enough to inspire him in the summer of 1862 to take the mail-boat from Leith to Reykjavik, not the easiest of voyages. We have no account of his travels, but any visit to Iceland at that time was an adventure. By the time of his return some weeks later he had become acquainted with the great Icelandic scholar Eiríkur Magnússon (1833–1913), who, bearing the manuscript of the latest version of the Bible in Icelandic, travelled back with Powell on his way to the Bible Society in London. Magnússon spent that Christmas with Powell at Nanteos.

For several years Powell and Magnússon corresponded, and they collaborated in the publication of two volumes titled *Icelandic Legends* (1864, 1866), totalling over a thousand pages. Magnússon was the translator, sending his work to Powell to improve his literal English. Powell's versions have been criticised in the past, but they are of the style of the age. The legends had to wait another century for a new translator. Powell must surely have paid not only for their publication but for the illustrations by Johann Zwecker, a German artist and book-illustrator based in London, whom he knew. The poor sales of the volumes didn't discourage him from further involvement in Icelandic matters.

These legends of Iceland should not be confused with the Icelandic sagas, the texts of which depend on medieval manuscripts. The legends or folk-tales were collected by Jón Árnason and published in Icelandic in two volumes, 1862 and 1864. Powell and Magnússon's English versions, *Legends of Iceland*, appeared remarkably soon after the originals. Powell would certainly have met Árnason during his 1862 visit, since Árnason was custodian of both the embryo National Library and National Museum of Iceland. The volumes are discussed in the Afternote to this chapter: George Powell as Author.

It was George's desire to dedicate the second volume

of the *Legends* to Swinburne that first brought the two men together to begin a burgeoning friendship. Algernon Swinburne was a friend of William Morris, the remarkable Victorian dynamo who gave so much to the Socialist movement and to the Arts and Crafts movement. Swinburne wrote to Powell to say that '[Morris] is as much interested as you are, though as ignorant as I am, concerning Icelandic matters. He is in my opinion, and in that of older and wiser men, one of the best poets of the time, and a great admirer of your work.' He also commented to Powell that, 'He is besides a Welshman, like yourself'. Morris owned a copy of *Legends of Iceland*, he studied Icelandic with Eiríkur Magnússon and wrote on Icelandic themes even before visiting the country in 1871 and again in 1873. There is no record that Powell ever met William Morris, although he knew some members of the Pre-Raphaelite movement in which Morris was deeply involved, and acquired a few of their artworks.

George Powell also became involved in Icelandic politics. Iceland at the time was part of Denmark's overseas empire, and was allowed a single elected representative in the Danish parliament. The unsalaried member in the 1860s was Jón Sigurđsson, for whom the Danish authorities made life seriously difficult. He is now Iceland's national hero, and for some years he depended on money from George Powell, ostensibly to subsidise Sigurđsson's scholarly work on the history of Iceland, but nothing came of that project. Magnússon described Powell as '[being] full of the most sympathetic enthusiasm for the cause of Icelandic Homerule [*sic*] and Jón Sigurđsson's classical patriotism.' 'I have decided to defeat the Danes,' were Powell's words, 'by enabling Sigurđsson to attent to his parliamentary business in spite of them.' Powell continued to work on a version (unpublished) of an Icelandic saga, and to add relevant books to his growing library. Unsurprisingly his name is better known in Iceland than in Wales.

Nor is it surprising that one of the most striking paintings in George's collection is the original and definitive portrait of Fjallkonan, the Icelandic Lady of the Mountains, wearing her crown of ice from which volcanic fire erupts. Fjallkonan is the feminine symbol of Icelandic identity, first brought to imaginative life in 1752 by the poet Eggert Ólafsson. Her image was created visually in the mid-nineteenth century by Powell's artist friend Johann Baptist Zwecker, following the instructions of Eiríkur Magnússon. Zwecker made a black-and-white image for Volume II of Powell and Magnússon's *Icelandic Legends* (1866); the watercolour original is among Powell's bequests to the nascent University College of Wales, Aberystwyth. Only recently did this original come to the attention of modern Icelandic scholars.

Eiríkur Magnússon described the picture in a letter to Jón Sigurđsson:

> The picture of the woman is to represent Iceland, thus she has a crown of ice on her head, from which fires erupt. On her shoulder is the raven, Iceland's most characteristic bird, Óðinn's ancient friend and the favourite of poets, a great and knowledgeable carrier of news. Over the seas flutters a seagull, but across the surf of time and history are borne rune-staves to the land and up into the embrace of the woman, and she has picked one of them up. This is intended as a symbol of our land of literature and history. It is night, with a starry sky and the moon up. Behind are mountains, moonlight on the ridges.

After his visits to Iceland in 1862 and Denmark in 1863, George went to Morocco the following year, and delighted in dressing as a Moroccan when back in Britain. Magnússon, who had hoped for his help in compiling an Icelandic dictionary, commented ruefully but sympathetically:

> [Powell's] intense love of music and art generally caused him to spend much of his time in travel, and sustained sedentary application to the somewhat dry work of lexicographical interpretation was not congenial to his ardent spirit.

While George's passion for Icelandic culture waned, music was a lifelong delight to him. We do not know how he learned to play the piano sufficiently well to give recitals in Cardiganshire for charity, but he had installed a Broadwood upright at Nanteos in 1860, and had become interested in opera. His 'Gleanings' volume includes three concert programmes for 1866, one at the Assembly Rooms under the presidency of W.T.R. Powell, and two others in the National School Room, at all of which Powell performed on the piano. He also presided on a fourth occasion, this time at the Aberystwyth Temperance Hall, but did not perform.

It was in 1866 that George had met the poet Algernon Swinburne (1837–1909), a fellow Etonian, and the two loved to reminisce about the beatings inflicted on them at school. Swinburne celebrated sado-masochism in his remarkable ode to 'Dolores, Our Lady of Pain'. One verse is enough to convey the poem's essence:

By the ravenous teeth that have smitten
 Through the kisses that blossom and bud,
By the lips intertwisted and bitten
 Till the foam has a savour of blood,
By the pulse as it rises and falters,
 By the hands as they slacken and strain,
I adjure thee, respond from thine altars,
 Our Lady of Pain...

... and so on for fifty-five stanzas. The wonder is that Swinburne was able to survive into a respectable old age.

It was inevitable that George's father would forbid the notorious Swinburne entry to Nanteos, so the pair rented a cottage in Cwm Rheidol for a while. Swinburne also enjoyed sea bathing at Aberystwyth. Two hundred and more letters written between the two friends from 1865 to 1879 survive; most are from Swinburne. Indeed, the eighteen-year-old George had himself already been forbidden from Nanteos in 1860, writing some time later to his friend Eiríkur Magnússon that he would not go there again 'henceforth and forever', though that promise was in the end too extreme.

Powell and Swinburne enjoyed discussing the works of the Marquis de Sade, of which Swinburne told Powell, 'My copy of his monstrous offspring is still in the hands of an Eton friend, who having been incessantly whipped during the rosy years of boyhood – rosy in bottom as in face – takes, I fear, a voluptuous interest in the Titanic flagellations which crown its pages.' When in 1868 Powell rented a seaside cottage at Étretat in Normandy for the two of them, he named it 'La Chaumière de Dolmancé', a name taken from de Sade's *La Philosophie dans le Boudoir*

(1795), a text which still has the capacity to horrify anyone who might stray on it by chance.

Guy de Maupassant, later famous as France's greatest writer of short stories, aged only sixteen at the time, gave a lurid description of the Étretat establishment, where he was shown albums of obscene photographs, taken in Germany, all of masculine subjects, and a mummified human hand used as a paperweight, no longer surviving among George's collection of curiosities. His visit was the result of his having swum to the rescue of Swinburne, who as we know enjoyed sea bathing but had ventured out too far from the beach. Maupassant recounted his visits, for he visited the cottage more than once, to the Goncourt brothers, whose account loses nothing in the repetition. Maupassant describes Nip, the tame monkey in the house, whose portrait by Zwecker has been lost. A later Maupassant story, 'L'Anglais d'Étretat', is a fictionalised version of his experiences:

> They had a way of seeing and understanding that made them seem like diseased visionaries, drunken with a poetry magical and perverse. [They] recounted Icelandic legends, translated by Mr Powell, of a gripping and terrible novelty.

Of Powell he says:

> He loved the supernatural, the macabre, the tortured, the intricate and every form of derangement.

Indeed it might be suggested that George Powell anticipated the Decadent movement of the 1890s, though he never lived to see it.

Not enough of George Powell's letters survive to allow

an extended biography, nor did he leave any diary. But another facet of his many-layered nature is revealed in a letter he wrote from Mayence (as the German city of Mainz was known in English), France, in 1870, when the French launched their catastrophic attack on Prussia. It shows that he visited wounded soldiers in hospitals and at railway stations, spending all he could afford on humanitarian relief. This must have led to his 1871 membership of a London committee which, on behalf of the Society of British Artists, arranged an exhibition to raise money for 'the Distressed Peasantry of France', whose misery had resulted from Napoleon III's folly and the resulting submission and humiliation of France.

George had planned to go to Bayreuth with Swinburne in 1867, though the scheme fell through. In 1876, however, he attended the first performances of Wagner's complete Ring cycle at Bayreuth, becoming well acquainted with the composer and his formidable wife Cosima, the illegitimate daughter of Franz Liszt. He also came to know Schumann's widow, Clara, as well as Offenbach and Liszt himself. The often-told tale that Wagner visited Nanteos and was inspired by its healing cup to compose his opera *Parsifal* is nonsense. Powell bought much published music as well as manuscripts of Gluck and Mendelssohn.

As early as 1861 Powell was corresponding with Sir Frederick Arthur Gore Ouseley, professor of music at Oxford, who became a good friend, and with his successor, Sir John Stainer, who acknowledged to Powell that it was his influence that had brought him to appreciate the music of Schumann. As well as giving generously to Ouseley's College of Church Music, George also supported Joseph Parry's School of Music in Swansea financially and with gifts of books, which eventually reverted to the University College at Aberystwyth when Parry was appointed to the chair of Music in 1874.

At some point in the 1860s Powell made his London home in the artistic enclave at 41, Mornington Crescent, where he must have kept most if not all of his books and *objets d'art*, at least until he inherited Nanteos in 1878, probably until his death. He lived a busy life in Town, attending theatres, concert halls and galleries, as well as London Zoo. Art was a major passion. In the 1870s he knew many Pre-Raphaelite artists and acquired some of their sketches, but oil-paintings of quality were usually more than his purse could bear. Dante Gabriel Rosetti in particular was expensive, but George did acquire one portrait sketch. He was friendly with the sibling painters Simeon and Rebecca Solomon, several of whose works he bought. Simeon Solomon knew many of the Pre-Raphaelite Brotherhood, and was a friend of Swinburne, for whose novel *Lesbia Brandon* he provided illustrations. Solomon's career went into steep decline when, in 1873, he was convicted in London of indecent exposure and then in Paris of soliciting men, though Powell did not cut him off entirely. Subsequently the artist descended into alcoholism and destitution, but following his death in 1905 his work never disappeared from view entirely, and has been exhibited on a number of occasions from 1906 onwards.

A 1929 study of the Victorian Romantics included a chapter on Simeon Solomon, and in later decades his reputation further revived, especially after the decriminalisation of homosexuality. In 1985 Birmingham Museum and Art Gallery mounted an exhibition, *Solomon:*

a Family of Painters, involving Simeon, his brother Abraham and their sister Rebecca. The curator asked Aberystwyth, not for any of Powell's three watercolours by Simeon, but for Rebecca Solomon's fine *The Wounded Dove*. The choice is easily explained; Simeon had had a fairly long and productive career, meaning there were many pictures available, whereas when Rebecca died aged only thirty-two her work was quickly forgotten, like that of other women artists, or subsumed by other artists; only a few of her paintings are known to have survived. As far as can be told, she specialised in narrative painting, with a strong inclination to feminist themes.

More recently, three of Powell's four watercolours by Simeon Solomon were loaned for the Tate's 2001 exhibition and printed in its catalogue, *Exposed: the Victorian Nude*. Studies have been published, and in 2017 works by Solomon from Powell's collection were shown at the Tate Britain exhibition, *Queer British Art 1861–1967*. The work illustrated in the photograph section, *Love Dreaming by the Sea*, is a good representative of his work in watercolour.

Seventy years ago the adjective 'queer' was used of men perceived as being homosexual. It now takes its place in the multiple categories of sexuality known as LGBTQ+ and 'queer' is perhaps an epithet to describe what we know of George Powell. He was certainly not a pursuer of women, though his short life did end with a brief marriage. The descriptions of his summer cottage given by both Guy de Maupassant and the Goncourt brothers in their journals are certainly lurid to the point of exaggeration, and there is no doubt that his taste in art tended to the homoerotic in his purchases of pictures and figurines. This, however, was by no means exclusively the case; there are a number of watercolours and figurines of young women.

Whatever may have been the nature of George Powell's private life, he made considerable efforts to contribute to cultural life in Aberystwyth, founding the Aberystwyth Literary Institute and Working Men's Club in 1867, to which he donated hundreds of books. He surely realised not only that he would have no child to inherit his collections, but that his cousin and heir William Beaumont Powell was not at all likely to appreciate them. From 1874 he made determined efforts to persuade Aberystwyth Town Council to create a public museum and library, to which he promised to give his own collections. But Aberystwyth, small town that it was, was wholly unable to finance such a venture adequately, and the project ran into the sands. Powell was deeply disappointed; in his book of 'Gleanings', the first thirty-eight pages are filled with cuttings from the local paper about his gifts of books to the town's Literary Institute and his failed project to create a home for his paintings and other collections. However, despite the disappointment, George would soon have a better idea.

The 'Gleanings' volume seems to have been compiled in 1881 from cuttings and other papers which George had kept for some years. The last pages are full of cuttings about Bayreuth and Wagner, with some still loose in the volume since all the pages had been filled. Another cutting lists donors to the restoration of Llanbadarn Fawr parish church. The list is headed by three names, Colonel Powell Nanteos, Sir Pryse Pryse, Gogerddan, and G.E.J. Powell, Esq., Nanteos – each gave two hundred pounds. He also assembled, in scores of volumes, an extraordinary miscellany of cuttings from periodicals, which he entitled 'Essays, Poems and Reviews'.

Aberystwyth Town Council's failure to cope with George Powell's offers did not blunt his generosity. Instead he turned to the University College of Wales, which had been established in 1872. It occupied the large seafront neo-Gothic hotel which had been built for but never used by travellers arriving on the railway from Machynlleth, which had opened in 1864. George wrote to Principal Thomas Charles Edwards offering the College not only his library but his art and music collections as well. In his own words:

> In my will, therefore, I had left to your University – as well as being quite the worthiest and most intelligent corporate body in my dear but benighted town – all I possessed 'of bigotry and virtue'.

Those words 'bigotry' and 'virtue' strike one as strange; what exactly did he mean – especially 'bigotry'?

Even before this actually happened, he had made a remarkable purchase which would be to the College's benefit. Shortly before his death in 1878, W.T.R. Powell had agreed that the trustees of the estate should sell land between Llanbadarn Fawr and Aberystwyth, including the Vicarage Field and the Archery Ground. The sale was held at the Talbot Hotel in Market Street, Aberystwyth, on 9 July in the same year, and George bought the two pieces of ground for £2,510, as reported in the *Cambrian News* of 12 July. After George's death, the Vicarage Field was sold, eventually becoming the University College's first sports ground.

As for George's gift of his collections to the College, it

was remarkable, and it was accepted, though it can hardly have been realised at the time how complex a responsibility this would be for a small college whose income was extremely fragile and its future far from certain. It must be remembered that it is unlikely that the principal or any of his staff would have seen any part of the collections, which were in London. In later retrospect it may have come to seem a never-ending and potentially expensive project. It became a matter of housing, cataloguing and day-to-day care and curating of thousands of books, a large music collection, one hundred and fifty paintings, drawings and prints, many sculptures and ceramics, a collection of five hundred coins and endless memorabilia – especially photographs, *cartes de visite,* sculptures, autographs, netsukes, miscellaneous curios and souvenirs of all kinds. There was simply no way the struggling College could have managed it all competently. Despite so many difficulties, however, the collections would surely have been scattered and forgotten but for the College's willing acceptance of George Powell's generosity, although without any accompanying endowment.

The root of the problem was that the real interest of the collection lay in its almost freakish diversity rather than the presence of any major treasures. It was certainly far more than simply a cabinet of curiosities. It represented the tastes of a gentleman-aesthete of multitudinous interests but comparatively limited means. The works of art George Powell bought included examples by Edward Burne-Jones, Dante Gabriel Rossetti and by his friends, Johann Zwecker, Wilhelm K mpel and the siblings Simeon and Rebecca Solomon, as well as two minor watercolours by Turner and minor works attributed to Constable and F.W.

Watts. Powell was also interested in the unusual subject of corporeal decay, and owned a series of five such studies. There is nothing in the collection which could be classed as pornographic (a favourite hobby of some Victorian gentlemen); if there had been, we can be sure it wouldn't have been allowed to reach the University College.

George took pride in having had many of the works of his contemporaries, including his friends K mpel and Zwecker, 'executed expressly for me'; clearly he saw himself as patron as well as collector. Those words come from Powell's unpublished catalogue of his art collection. He valued it as his own 'minute, careful and patient research', optimistically describing some of his items as 'of incalculable artistic value'. He follows with the words that the collection must 'as dreams often take the place of reality – now take the reality of my dreams.'

Apart from the paintings and sketches, George Powell also picked up a number of figurines in ceramic and bronze, as well as pots and plaques of varied origins. Then there were the Japanese netsukes, tiny ivory sculptures which are still popular with many collectors. One is a three-dimensional miniature ivory sculpture, the others are all of the type known as mirror-lid (kagamibuta-netsuke), part ivory, part metal, believed to be nineteenth-century work.

Also in the collection are a number of Japanese Satsuma bowls, which to judge by today's on-line prices must be among the collection's most valuable items. He also bought a gallimaufry of other objects: coins, a Viennese tea-set which he believed wrongly to have been associated with Mozart, mineral specimens from Iceland, Persian needlework, a pair of Canadian snowshoes, a cast of Mendelssohn's hand, a crystal casket which once contained a supposed fragment of Schumann's coffin (how, if genuine, did that come about?) – the variety is extraordinary to the point of bewilderment. Was this, along with the autographs and letters, and of course the books, perhaps collecting for collecting's sake? It all looks like the acquisition of virtually any exotic, shiny object which appealed to his magpie nature.

Indeed, collecting must have taken up a considerable part of George's life; buying from shops, purchasing at auctions (no evidence, but likely), assembling and cataloguing, as well as his frequent travels. But there is evidence that, although in his twenties George could be the soul of generosity, by his thirties he was finding it less easy to help others on the scale, for example, on which he had supported his Icelandic friends, or Ouseley's School of Church Music.

For many years after George's death, the College would not have an Art Department. Benign neglect and possible losses seemed inevitable. Matters improved with the involvement of Professor H.J. Fleure, a former student at Aberystwyth who was a senior member of staff from 1908 till 1930. This great scholar saw the general cultural value of the collection, ensured more display facilities and appreciated the interest and value of George Powell's bequest. He called, optimistically but in vain, for the appointment of a full-time curator of the College's collections. But even the establishment of the College museum did not give much space or attention to the Powell collection as such.

David Tinker's appointment in the 1960s as the first head of the College's Arts and Crafts, originally within the Education Department, brought new attention to the collection's problems, including Tinker's proposal to sell some items to reinforce the collection's conservation and consistency. Much of the Powell collection might have been disposed of if this policy had been adopted, especially perhaps as David Tinker's rigorously modernistic tastes were absolutely the opposite of Powell's. However, once the present University Department of Fine Arts was properly established, adequately staffed and eventually accommodated in 1993 in the splendid Edward Davies building, appreciation of the George Powell collection has become a matter of pride. It was properly catalogued, and is often drawn on for exhibitions both in the department's galleries and further afield. A vital initiative was the mounting in 1978 of an exhibition curated by Moira Vincentelli, who followed this with two important articles on the history of the College's collections. She brought about an improvement in the conditions of the Powell bequest by the sale of a few of his Japanese netsuke figures.

George Powell's gifts of books are in the care of the University's Hugh Owen Library; they number well over two thousand volumes, in addition to much printed music and a number of manuscripts. The collection is far more personal and idiosyncratic than what is usually found in so many gentry libraries, with their serried ranks of bound periodicals, encyclopaedias, law reports and sets of classic works of history and literature. Like the art collection, it gives an insight into Powell's dilettante intellect; it is an eclectic assemblage – some manuscripts, and a wide variety of English and French literature, travel books, art, Icelandic sagas and much musical material. Perhaps the most valuable volumes are the Warburton edition of Shakespeare's plays published in 1747. They were once owned by Dr Samuel Johnson, and were used not only for his edition of Shakespeare but for his great English dictionary; the volumes have many of Johnson's manuscript notes. George paid fifteen guineas for the set in 1862. This seems quite a remarkable purchase for a twenty year old.

The first scholar to draw attention to George Powell's library was the late Richard Brinkley of the University's Hugh Owen Library, who in 1971 mounted an exhibition of his books, music and manuscripts in the Great Hall gallery at the University's Arts Centre. The exhibition catalogue gave a brief note of Powell's life, while the exhibits were listed under Powell's friendship with Swinburne, other friends, some valuable books and Powell's Icelandic interest. Brinkley also wrote a pioneer article on Powell for the *Anglo-Welsh Review*.

There are of course many books in the collection which can be called standard reading, but some more unusual subjects also appear. Powell was clearly interested in mental illness, diseases in general, demonology and witchcraft, as well as explorations of alternative forms of marriage. A *Book of Wonderful Characters* (1869) deals with men whose eccentricities derive from genetic or behavioural problems. These deviations from the norm are what renders them interesting, rather than any more 'normal' achievements. But the appearance of a book was certainly enough to attract Powell. His purchase of a 1567 edition of the Roman Catholic missal should not lead one to suppose him particularly curious about Catholicism. Rather, he would have been struck by the splendid ornate binding, and in particular by the fore-edge painting

One might surmise that some of his books were gifts from friends; certainly Swinburne gave him an edition of English metrical psalms by a number of authors published by the Stationers' Company in 1620. It includes some tunes, and the title page has a fine ornamental surround. Another even more attractive little book is a Dutch breviary of the fourteenth/fifteenth century. It was obviously acquired as a curiosity rather than an intellectual resource. He had also picked up a Papal Bull.

Surprisingly, George never commissioned a good bookplate, though one of his artist friends would surely have obliged; Simeon Solomon designed a most attractive one for Mary Gladstone, the Grand Old Man's daughter. As it was, George's choice of bookplate was plain to the point of being ugly; he was also fond of signing his name on title pages. However, he took much trouble over cataloguing his book collection. He bought a fine leather-bound ledger, and hundreds of his books are listed, page after page in a fine copperplate hand. He used red ink for every capital letter in both book and authorial name, which must have been really troublesome; one is tempted to believe that he hired someone to do the work. The catalogue does not represent his whole collection, and it would not be easy to compare it with the library itself, but it does demonstrate a capacity for taking pains, whether or not the script is all his own work. Towards the end of the volume he listed his picture collection: portraits, heads and figures etc., watercolours, oils, sketches, landscapes, illustrative paintings and some of Zwecker's illustrations for the two volumes of Icelandic legends.

Thomas Lloyd has pointed out that George Powell's library, although reflecting several of his personal interests, especially Icelandic studies and music, seems to have been acquired at random rather than with specific aims in mind. The books were probably bought mostly in London and almost certainly kept at his Mornington Crescent home there, without any known overlap with the Nanteos library. Moving all his collections to Aberystwyth must have been quite an undertaking.

George collected photographs of his many friends and acquaintances, surviving in an album of *cartes de visite* now in the National Library of Wales, although some at least are unlikely to have been used as visiting cards; one shows a dog, several others young children. There are various pictures of Eiríkur Magnússon and of his wife, and a number of famous names appear, some of which he acquired by writing to the individuals concerned: H.W. Longfellow, Ernest Renan, Franz Liszt, Hector Berlioz, Alexandre Dumas, Théophile Gautier and Gustave Doré. There's little doubt that George was something of what was known in the eighteenth century as a 'tuft-hunter'.

During the 1870s there are references in the Swinburne correspondence to George's health, which may well have been deteriorating; it has been suggested that he may have suffered from some form of the venereal diseases so rampant at the time, but there is no evidence whatever. Alcohol consumption or the use of laudanum may well have been problems, but again – no evidence, none. Despite bouts of illness, he remained a London resident even after his father's death in 1878. One newspaper report of his death says specifically that 'he did not take up his residence in the family mansion... but occupied his time largely in travelling'. The local newspapers have hardly any records of his appearance at Nanteos before he served as the county's High Sheriff for a year in 1881, a ceremonial position which he abhorred.

He described the experience in a comical letter to Swinburne.

> You will, I'm sure, be glad to hear that my business at Cardigan, as high sheriff, went off splendidly. Never had such a 'get up' and 'turn out' been seen in the county. Without being in the least degree gaudy, everything was soberly splendid, as I used only two colours for my liveries, black and white or – as the case of the trumpeters – black and silver. I used violet for the hammer-cloth and lining of carriage. I had only *two* accidents during the whole proceedings. The first was with my sword, and long white want (a horrible instrument). The former fell at the Church gate, as I got out of the carriage, out of its scabbard, with a hideous clatter, and the want fell between my legs, thus betraying me into an undignified tumble, which even the prompt help of my footmen almost failed to redeem. However, I managed to receed [*sic*] Mr Bowen, the pro-judge, into church, with appropriate majesty. My second misadventure was worse. On the next day, I had the Grand Jury to lunch, most of whom were acquaintances, and kept them beyond after open court-time. Consequently Judge Thesiger (who had broken etiquette by taking my carriage without my leave on Saturday eve to spend Sunday in a neighbouring county – a fearful breach of good manners – and thus avoid the assize sermon) thought fit to lecture me on Monday morning about my 'lack of respect'.

There seems to be no records of any events during that year, apart from that appearance as High Sheriff at the County Assizes. There are however frequent reports of his many gifts to the University College. In spite of the evidence in the previous paragraph, George Powell was in residence late in 1878, because his name appears in a Nanteos game book. His apparent distaste for shooting had given way to limited pursuit of pheasants and partridges. In November 1880 he was again shooting on the estate.

Powell's lack of interest in the Nanteos estate which provided his income is attested by an item in the *Cambrian News* for 17 March 1882, a report of a conversation between an unnamed landowner and a correspondent represented by the initials P.W. In what may have been a dialogue of his own sardonic invention, 'P.W.' was strongly critical of the landlord class:

> Myself: Do you think a landlord is doing his duty to his tenants, who leaves the whole management of his estate in the hands of his agents, as is the case at *Nanteos*?
> Landowner: Mr Powell's tastes run into art and literature.
> Myself: What I ask is, whether he discharges his duty to his tenants by leaving them entirely in the hands of the agent?
> Landowner: Surely you do not think a landlord ought to manage his own estates. The drudgery would be unbearable.

The last comment is indeed revealing.

In May 1881, after completing his year as Cardiganshire's High Sheriff, George Powell married Dinah T. Harries, of Beach Cottage, Goodwick, Pembrokeshire, described in the marriage certificate as being a minor (under twenty-one years old). Her father is described as a 'captain in the Merchant Service'. They married not in Dinah's parish but in George's parish church of St Matthew in London; was that possibly to convenience Dinah's father, who as a ship's captain would have been a frequent visitor to London? The marriage comes as a surprise, since George had shown no romantic interest in women's company, and his artistic taste tended to the homoerotic. But George may already have been a sick man by the time of his wedding; indeed, the marriage may possibly have been arranged for his care, rather than with any prospect of begetting an heir. His surviving letters frequently complain of various illnesses, including diarrhoea and colic.

The couple were warmly welcomed on their arrival in Aberystwyth, and the Nanteos tenants presented them with a massive silver *épergne* or table centrepiece two feet high, costing £70. But George Powell died suddenly on 17 October 1882, just over a year after the wedding. He had been expected to take the chair at an Aberystwyth concert on that day. The *Cambrian News* attributed his death to 'a violent cramp'. His loss was sincerely mourned by Algernon Swinburne, himself at the time entering his late period of respectability. In memorial verses he described George as his 'friend of many a season', 'an ardent spirit', 'a gentle heart and true'.

Among the many mourners – tenants, tradesmen, gentry and two Baptist ministers – who filled Llanbadarn Fawr church at the funeral were Principal Thomas Charles Edwards of the University College of Wales, with two professors and three students, representing the College's debt to so generous a donor. Aberystwyth Grammar School was also strongly represented.

George Powell's will confirmed his many gifts to the University College, and made generous allowance for his widow Dinah. She soon took herself off to the United States, where she remarried in 1885 with a Mr Ulysses Whildin, but apparently was still able to enjoy a reduced pension from Nanteos until her death in 1942. Her descendants retain to this day a few items she brought with her to the US; they like to refer to George as 'Lord Powell'. Mrs Whildin was still occasionally corresponding with Mrs Margaret Powell at least as late as 1937. But quite the most remarkable of George's financial bequests was that of £100 a year to Miss Margaretta Lewis – the very woman who had brought a case for breach of promise against George's father, W.T.R. Powell, nearly twenty years earlier. This does seem to be an acknowledgement of sympathy for her predicament. She died unmarried in 1892.

A more lasting touch of George's revenge on his father's name is to be seen in the great east window of Llanbadarn Fawr church, given by George in memory of his mother and his sister, whose name is misspelt Harriot – without mention of his father. The central figure of Christ is flanked on both sides by musician-angels, each with a different instrument, reflecting George's own passion for music. Yet further evidence of George's detestation of his father is the fact that he commissioned no memorial of any kind in his memory. W.T.R. Powell is commemorated in Llanbadarn Fawr only in a stained-glass window of 1884, along with his cousins Cornelius Powell and W.E. Phelp. This window was paid for by Cornelius's son Richard Powell.

Living in London, travelling to Iceland, Belgium, France, Denmark, Austria, Germany, Spain, Germany and north Africa, a passion for music, collecting books, art and memorabilia – all these replaced in George Powell the more usual gentry lusts for hunting, shooting, fishing, heavy drinking and gluttonous feasting. His bequests to the University College of Wales, Aberystwyth, though limited in their crude financial value, are as a collection unique of their kind; an effort has been made to reflect their variety in illustrating this volume. Whatever his personal weaknesses may have been, and despite his scant attention to the Nanteos estate and his indifference to Cardiganshire politics, to me at least George seems by far the most interesting and in many ways likeable man of the whole Powell family, as far as one can possibly judge.

Afternote 1: The Aberystwyth University Coin Collection

It is sad that Aberystwyth University's historic coin collection, of which George Powell's collection was the first deposit, is not available for public view. Sad, but unsurprising, since the cost of a secure cabinet and place might match or well outrun the collection's value, though that is not insubstantial. Equally sad is that George Powell's original collection, unlisted by him, wasn't catalogued when given to the then University College of Wales in the 1880s. Since then it endured the vicissitudes of Powell's other bequests until the coins were listed in 1975–81. By that time other gifts of coins had been made to the college and themselves melded into the collection. The list includes a large number of Roman coins used by the university's History Department for teaching Roman history; this may also be true of some of the medieval and early modern English coins. Obviously, too, the fine 1887 collection of Queen Victoria's coinage of that Jubilee year could have had nothing to do with Powell, who died in 1882. On the other hand, I would hazard a guess that the few French gold coins of Napoleon III may well have come from George Powell's hands. He might, too, have owned the Charles I silver groat of Cardiganshire silver, which would certainly have appealed to him. But one can only guess.

My warmest thanks to Dr Eryn White of Aberystwyth's History and Welsh History Department, who put me on the trail of the coins, and to Ms Julie Archer of the university's Archives and Records, who kindly provided me with a copy of the list of the university's collection, and who explained the background to me.

Afternote 2: George Powell as Author

Like many an adolescent poet, George was keen to see his work in print, and had the means to publish them. Still only eighteen, and apparently staying in Brussels, he sent two collections to John Cox, a competent Aberystwyth printer in Pier Street. His own name is not present in either book; he used the name Miölnir, Nanteos. He gives a teasing reference to his choice of name in the preface to the second volume of verse:

> There has been much wonder expressed concerning my nom-de-plume. It is one I have used a long time, in writing articles in Magazines and Newspapers. I do not see that it needs explanation. So for a little longer I intend to mystify my readers, by using it without explanation. So far I will tell them – it is Swedish. It has a meaning, which formerly was remarkably apropos, but which is not now, owing to the different style of writing to which it is applied. I have an affection for it, as it once worked in my hands a considerable reform...

Whatever that may mean.

The epilogue to the first volume claims that the poems are 'exercises, not models; as foot lights, not as stars'; 'I fear me [your judgment] will be hard tried, but as I have amply apologized, I don't really care.' There is little that is original in the poems; the titles are enough: 'A Fever Vision', 'Fairies', 'The Rose and the Violet', 'Dying', and so on. There is an attempt at whimsical humour, 'Agriculture, by a Facetious Farmer':

> I planted once a wise old man,
> And up there came some sage;
> There's more of *this*, than *that* now in
> This artificial age.
>
> I planted a cigar also,
> And up there came a weed:
> A very natural consequence
> Of such a nasty weed.

And so on. Powell deeply regretted having published this frivolous poem.

The second volume followed quickly on the first, and though the contents are similar, at one hundred and sixty pages this book is more ambitious than was the first at sixty. The first ten poems are dedicated to his aunt, Julia Phelp; the next eighteen to 'my very dear friend Claude Frederick Fox Chawner', an Anglican clergyman, with a separate preface from Brussels dated 1 March 1861, apologising for delay.[1] There follows a section dedicated to 'Professor Longfellow... as a token of my sincere and profound admiration of his great genius'.

'Part the Fourth', another twelve poems, is dedicated simply to 'J.H.M.', with an intriguingly honest preface:

---

1 The Rev. Chawner was rector of Bletchingley, Redhill, Surrey, where George Powell stayed on at least one occasion.

> I had originally intended that this fourth part should consist, chiefly, of an 'Idyl' [*sic*] 'Eleanora'. I undertook the poem – which was a romance of Aberystwith Castle – and carried it to some length, but became disgusted with it (it was miserably weak and far too melodramatic).

In the epilogue, he regrets his attempts at humour in his first volume, but as for the rest, 'I cherish them, as one would cherish sickly and unsightly infants.' The reference to Aberystwyth castle (George's spelling of the name was common at the time) is intriguing. This is the only reference in all his works and papers to use of a possible Welsh topic, and clearly it came to nothing.

Finally, there is an addendum, the foreword to which George dated Friday, 20 December 1861, without naming a place. Last in the volume comes an elegy to Albert the Prince Regent, who had died six days earlier. Altogether it is not surprising that George published no more poetry. It doesn't seem appropriate to quote more from the verses; how many of us as adolescents would have taken the chance to publish our own juvenile efforts had we the resources and social status of George Powell? A third volume, *Quodlibet* ('what you will'), also printed by Cox, is so rare that I have been unable to see a copy.

Instead, George's imagination was captured by the culture of Iceland. Following his visit there, his friendship with Eiríkur Magnússon resulted in the collaborative publication of two volumes of *Icelandic Legends* in 1864 and 1866, quite an achievement for a man still in his early twenties. The title pages both acknowledge that the legends had been collected by Jón Árnason (1819–88), to whom George paid fulsome tribute for his work of thirty years collecting a great number of tales, which he published in two volumes in Leipzig in 1862 and 1866. Together they total 1,300 pages. Árnason was librarian at Reykjavik Cathedral and secretary to the bishop, eventually becoming the National Librarian and curator of the National Museum.

It is plain to see that European scholars preferred the study of the early Icelandic sagas, which survived from the medieval period in manuscript, to the oral tales collected in the nineteenth century by Árnason, since there were no further efforts to publish new translations for a century. When, in 1972, the folklore scholar Jacqueline Simpson published *Icelandic Folktales and Legends*, she used only the first three chapters of Árnason's 1862 volume to fill one hundred and eighty pages. Her comments on Powell and Magnússon's work recognises their effort 'to offer a representative range of material', but she observes that their work is 'stylistically most unsatisfactory, being full of repetitiveness, circumlocutions and pomposity'. These are faults for which Powell, not Magnússon, would be blamed if true, but comparison suggests that Simpson overstates her case.

It's possible to look at Simpson's style alongside Powell's by comparing several tales which occur both in her volume of 1972 and Powell's of 1864: 'Father of eighteen elves', 'Murder will Out', 'The Shepherdess (and the Trolls)' and 'Gryla'. I cannot comment on their closeness to the Icelandic originals, but in the first three stories the two translations are remarkably similar in both narrative details and length. Repetition and circumlocution hardly occur, while pomposity is simply attributable to the mid-Victorian English natural to George Powell. 'Gryla' is different; it is hardly a tale at all, but simply what Árnason was told was the nature of this particular troll. The two versions are very different; Simpson's is more detailed, while Powell's is more of a précis. Simpson's work is certainly closer in its abruptness to the style so common to international folk-tales.

There is no dedicatee in Powell's first volume of the *Legends*, but the second names both Lord Dufferin and Algernon Charles Swinburne, Esq. Dufferin (Frederick Hamilton-Temple-Blackwood), Governor-General of Canada at the time the *Legends* were published, was the author of a remarkably successful and amusing travel book, *Letters from High Latitudes*, describing his 1856 visit to Iceland and some Norwegian islands. The book was long in print, and in several languages, and obviously known to George Powell; it may well have been part of the inspiration of his own visit to Iceland in 1862. The dedication doesn't imply any personal acquaintance with Dufferin, but George would certainly have written to ask permission to dedicate the book to him, as he would have written to Longfellow for the dedication of some of his poems.

Quod-libet (Aberystwyth: J. Cox, 1860).

Poems, by Miölnir Nanteos (Aberystwyth: J. Cox, 1860).

Poems, by Miölnir Nanteos, second series (Aberystwyth: J. Cox, 1861).

8

The Last of the Powells of Nanteos

THE CHILDLESS GEORGE Powell was succeeded by his father's cousin, William Beauclerk Powell (1835–1911). He was a man of whom we know comparatively little compared with previous owners of Nanteos. His father Richard Powell had married Harriet Wynne of Peniarth, the great Meirionnydd estate, and appears to have lived a quiet life in Aberystwyth. In 1864 their son William Beauclerk, who had been an officer of the Leicestershire Militia, married Anna Maria Lewis, daughter of a cousin of the Pryses of Gogerddan; the marriage took place at Strata Florida church, though neither was domiciled in the parish of Caron. One son was born in 1870, Edward Athelstan Lewis Powell.

Such were the social changes from the middle of the nineteenth century that William Beauclerk could never have expected to live at the social or political level of his Nanteos predecessors. The general elections of 1858, 1867 and 1885 saw the breaking of the Tory grip on Wales and the growth of democracy, moving in tandem with the growth of Nonconformity, and the beginning of compulsory education for all in 1870. The creation of county councils in 1889 completed the political sidelining of the Welsh gentry, depriving them of the control of local government and politics they had once monopolised. They were left to enjoy their social status, and their hunting, shooting and fishing to the extent that shrinking estates and resources allowed.

Ownership of agricultural land had given guaranteed access to power and social influence, but it had never been a guarantee of wealth, which was often more readily found in minerals (coal, iron, lead), in trade and investment, but best of all in ownership of urban land, where rentals were (and are) much more profitable. Consider how the Mostyn estate and family have profited from the ownership of much of Llandudno, and the Meyricks of Bodorgan from their investment in Bournemouth. True, Nanteos had a considerable stake in Aberystwyth, but so did Gogerddan, and the little town was never wealthy enough to support both.

Successive owners of Nanteos had found themselves mired in mortgage debt while obliged to meet the expectations of marriageable daughters in need of dowries, as well as family members and servants in need of pensions. A gentleman was expected to live open-handedly, but this became more difficult as the century wore on. After 1870, royalties from lead-mining, which had been valuable to Nanteos as to Gogerddan and Trawsgoed, fell away quickly to very little, then nothing. Land had to be sold, and sold it was, from 1861 onwards in the case of Nanteos.

W.T.R. Powell continued selling in 1873 and 1878. George Powell's four-year tenure saw no sales, but the process had to go on, and there were further sales in

1884, 1892 and 1897, enabled by the Settled Land Act of 1882, which allowed the sale of land without reference to previous settlements. By 1910 more than two-thirds of all the Nanteos land had been sold at auction, even then leaving a mortgage debt of £30,000. So these were not good times for the estate, and there was little in the way of tree-planting or other developments. Farmhouses on the estate were often criticised by the local sanitary inspector for their poor condition.

Nevertheless, to read the local press one might imagine that in the 1880s little had changed at Nanteos or many other major houses in rural Wales. Hunting continued, involving the Nanteos Harriers or the Nanteos Foxhounds, balls were held, ploughing matches and agricultural shows took place, Christmas meat was distributed to workers' households, estate tenants and staff attended Christmas junketings, where there would be hearty eating, followed by speeches, songs and a poem in Welsh by the Nanteos gardener. The singing of 'Hen Wlad fy Nhadau' sometimes concluded these occasions.

There was a special gathering of friends and tenants for the 1891 coming-of-age of Edward Powell. At the festivities Edward delivered the first paragraph of his speech in Welsh, and promised to improve his fluency. His mother briefly addressed the assembly in Welsh, and it appears that she was fluent, hardly surprising in a member of the Peniarth family. One tenant was reported, while praising the family of the day, as remembering 'quite a different regime at Nanteos to the present'. He could not forget the time, when he was required to transact any business on going to Nanteos, being asked 'What do you want?', answering in Welsh, 'I want to see the Colonel (i.e. W.T.R.

Powell).' The reply would be, 'I know nothing about him; go home.' Tenants had become readier to use Welsh even on such a formal occasion.

The press report also carried a long list of birthday presents, including a horse from the tenants and at least two gold watches. As for Edward Powell, though he never mastered Welsh, he didn't want to alienate his tenants. In later years, when he wanted to thank a Mr Joel for his good work in preparing a monument to his dead son Billy Powell, he had someone translate into Welsh a moving letter of appreciation, and then signed it himself.

In 1891, William Beauclerk Powell assumed for a twelvemonth the expensive appointment of High Sheriff of the county, and his son Edward joined him on the local magistrates' bench. In retrospect, William Beauclerk seems to have been a natural candidate for gently running down the estate while maintaining a semblance of its former life. Having had only one child, he had therefore no worries about dowries for daughters, or having to purchase education and careers for second sons.

The 1881 Census shows Edward to have been one of twenty-five boarders at 'a school for little boys' at Tanllwyfan in Denbighshire. From there he went on to Rugby and Oxford. At some point Edward decided on a military career and joined the Leicestershire regiment (a long-standing family attachment), becoming a lieutenant before retiring in 1901. The date of Edward's Army enlistment is not known; the regimental record-keeper has little knowledge of him, but his other interests are clear. He loved breeding Welsh terriers, and was a skilled and enthusiastic horseman, enjoying his fine Arab steed; he spoke dismissively in a letter of 'Welsh Cobs & suchlike vermin'. He would have been astonished had he been able to foresee the extraordinary future success of the Welsh Cob.

While still in the Army, Edward married Margaret Pryse of Gogerddan on 4 February 1897, in Penrhyncoch church. She was nine years older than her husband, who was twenty-seven; the age difference may help to explain why only one child was born of their marriage. The list of wedding gifts was phenomenal, but while the tenants of Gogerddan presented a huge silver punchbowl, the Nanteos tenants had been asked for a Raleigh motor car, which would have been one of the earliest in the district. The problem is that Raleigh (now best known for its motorcycles and bicycles) appear not to have manufactured a car until 1899 – two years later. I haven't solved this conundrum.

By 1907, if not earlier, Edward had become a member of the Cardiganshire County Council for Llanilar. He and his wife were living at the Nanteos dower house, Rhydyfirian, with two servants. Their only child, the little boy William George Edward Pryse Wynne Powell, born in 1899 and known as Billy or 'Ick' to his parents, was away at school in Aldershot. In 1911 William Beauclerk Powell was still living at the mansion with his wife and six servants. But the couple both died that December, William Beauclerk on the fifth and his wife two days later; both were seventy-eight years old. Unusually there is no memorial to them inside the church, only a simple gravestone in the churchyard. Previous owners of Nanteos back to 1666 have memorials inside the church.

The outbreak of war in August 1914 would prove catastrophic for the Powells of Nanteos, as for so many other once great estates. Although Edward had retired from the Army and was forty-three when hostilities started, he insisted on rejoining the Leicesters in 1914. An August 1915 letter from their Patrington base in Yorkshire did not promise well: 'I am on the sick list today. My rheumatism is very bad and in addition my legs have chafed quite raw and I am all done up in bandaging. I hope before long to be made regimental transport officer in which case I should be mounted. The marching (especially in this heat) is rather too much for me… I am very much afraid I shall not be sent abroad, as the "Vets" [doctors], whenever I mention it, seem to think that I am not physically…' at which point the rest of the letter is missing.

Despite those worries, in March 1916 he was sent via Bombay to Mesopotamia, now Iraq, where there was much serious fighting. The Ottoman Empire had been dragged into the Great War by Germany late in 1914. No official record seems to survive of Powell's service there, but his wife Margaret kept a number of his letters home. Greeting her as 'My darling old Meazle' or 'old fish', he often lamented the routine boredom of his work, with frequent expressions of his love for Margaret and his dogs, and his occasional fears of post-war conditions: tax, lack of servants and low morale. He admitted that, 'All other people's [letters] are so depressing as to the state of affairs in England.' As with all soldiers abroad, mail was almost as important as food. Several of Margaret's letters might arrive at once, then nothing for weeks. Edward seems to have written every day whenever possible, but a week's writings might be part of a single letter, since post was not collected every day. While attempting to keep a stiff upper lip, it's obvious that he missed his wife terribly, writing once, 'If ever I do get back to you all I want is never to part again.' In January 1917 he reported that 'the other day, two English Red X nurses [arrived] on one of the ships. I did not see them but I believe they were gazed upon as an extraordinary spectacle. They soon went back of course.' Such was the nature of desert service; a soldier might not see a woman of his own country for a year or more. Nursing sick soldiers in Mesopotamia would have been carried out by male orderlies.

Worst of all was the climate. For example, in an undated letter Edward wrote:

> ... a pouring wet day today, so the move into trenches was postponed 24 hours but the wretched transport had started so there was some confusion & discomfort. You have no conception what the going is like in wet weather here. The sand that blinds & clothes you in the hot weather turns to knee-deep binding clay in wet and so slippery that even mules can hardly stand and frequently go down under a burden. France must be bad even on hard roads but here – where there are no roads of course and no stone at all, it must be much worse, but thank God that terrible sun and the flies are down and if one can only avoid ague and chill from wet clothes, I hope to struggle through it all right. Anyway so far I prefer it to the hot weather and sleepless nights.

There was occasional relief: he mentions jackal shooting and a gymkhana, the latter a distant reminder that many of the Allied soldiers in Mesopotamia were Indians.

Edward Powell's elderly (for a serving soldier) status did not keep him from the Mesopotamian battlefront against the Turks. Back home in Patrington, Yorkshire, at Easter 1918, he wrote: 'I well remember *last* Easter Sunday. The battle of Beled Station and how much I was thinking of you and Ick [i.e. Billy]… We were under fire from 8.40am till dark after having marched all the previous night. Lots more I could tell you and shall never forget.' After fifteen wretched months in 'Messpot as they call this hateful wilderness of desolation', he was sent back to Patrington, having served the fifteen months without a break. I cannot discover when he was demobilised. He brought back with him an (apparently undiagnosed) ailment contracted in Mesopotamia from which he suffered for the rest of his life. But the end of the war brought the bitterest blow of all.

*

Young Billy Powell had gone to Eton, and would normally have stayed on until 1918. But the war intervened, and aged seventeen he joined the Welsh Guards, quickly becoming a second lieutenant. In August 1918 he was sent to north-east France, and on 6 November he was shot while leading an attack on a German machine-gun post at Bouvignies, dying of his wounds three days later. The account of the attack in the regimental history of the Welsh Guards shows persuasively that rumours that he had been shot by his own men are not true, although of course the regimental history would not readily have admitted the possibility. In retrospect it is certainly shocking that such young and inexperienced men were sent on such suicidal missions when 'everyone' knew the war was virtually over. Powell is buried in the British cemetery at Maubeuge. Local tradition maintains that the Nanteos household was celebrating the news of the Armistice of 11 November when the news of

Billy's death reached them. However it was not announced in the local press until 22 November.

A memorial service for Billy Powell was held in Llanbadarn Fawr church on 8 January 1921, probably the occasion of the unveiling of a tablet on the south chancel wall, commemorating him as 'A very Gallant Welsh Gentleman'. On 31 May 1922 Lord Ystwyth (i.e. Matthew Lloyd-Davies of Tan-y-bwlch) unveiled a memorial cross to the dead heir of Nanteos at Southgate, the point where the road from Aberystwyth diverges in three directions, one for Aberaeron, one for Devil's Bridge, the third for Pontrhydfendigaid. For Edward Powell the loss of his only son must have been the last straw. The Earl of Lisburne noted in his diary for 18 January 1922:

> Travelled down to Crosswood. A most lovely warm day. Poor Ned Powell also travelling down. He lives a wretched life at Nanteos without a penny and I am afraid drinks hard.

Heartbroken and sick, Edward Powell died on 26 March 1930, leaving his widow Margaret as landlady of Nanteos. Local tradition maintains that she had a long-standing affair with Matthew Lloyd-Davies of Tan-y-bwlch, but in the nature of such matters it is not easy to say what was going on. Certainly Mrs Powell greatly enjoyed entertaining company, lonely as her life was otherwise. She is remembered in north Cardiganshire as quite a formidable lady, and particularly for her ear-trumpet. She did all she could to maintain the dignity of her shrunken realm, and would for example be ready to welcome groups of visitors, whether adults or children. She strongly resisted the compulsory purchase by the local council of the land between the estate and Aberystwyth, on which the Penparcau suburb was to be built. Her particular contribution to Nanteos history is to be found in the story of the Nanteos Cup, given below.

Wads of letters survive from the years 1931–34 dealing with the affairs of the Nanteos estate and its inheritance after Edward Powell's death. So complex were matters that cases were prepared for judicial hearings. Margaret Powell's brother George Pryse-Saunders wrote to his sister ('Dear Missy') frequently at this time about the difficulties involved in winding up the whole affair. Incidentally, he mentioned the dreadful agricultural depression of the time, writing in June 1932, 'We are having rent days just now but I do not know whether we shall get any money in as things are very bad with farmers all round... prices of all stock are very low.'

The 1939 outbreak of war must have seemed ominous to Mrs Powell, by then nearly eighty. But she made great efforts to maintain a tradition of hospitality. Griffith Evans of Lovesgrove wrote early in January 1942 to thank her for her generous present to him and his family, saying, 'I am still lost in wonder at the veritable hosts you fed on Boxing Day, both in the Dining room and at the Back.'

In the absence of an heir, Margaret Powell was secure in her tenure of Nanteos for life after her husband's death. But long before 1930 there would have been much speculation about what might be the eventual fate of the mansion and the remainder of the estate. Captain J. Hext Lewes RN, of Llanllŷr, a cousin of Margaret Powell by the Pryse connection, told the 2001 history of Nanteos that he had had expectations, but realised in 1936 that he would be unable to meet the death duties which would be levied at Mrs Powell's death, especially as death duties had not yet been paid after Edward Powell's death; indeed, there was still £37,000 owing in 1954.

Margaret Powell died on 21 March 1951, aged eighty-nine, and was buried – without any kind of memorial inscription – with other Powells outside the east end of Llanbadarn Fawr church. Speculation about the Nanteos inheritance was rife. Several months went by before a housemaid found a will, secreted under the lining paper of a drawer. Arguments then began as to whether the will was valid. It was dated, signed and witnessed, as a will should be, but who were the witnesses? It transpired that they were two French nuns, kindly accommodated at Nanteos during the war at the request of the Catholic Archbishop of Cardiff, Michael McGrath. In addition there were two unwitnessed codicils, one of which named two possible successors to the estate. One was Captain Hext Lewes, the other was Betty Garnon Williams, who in 1945 had married James S. Mirylees, an officer in the Royal Corps of Signals. To who exactly she was a cousin is not clear in any available sources, nor have I been able to discover the nature of the relationship. The validity of the will was disputed by three Pryse cousins of Mrs Powell and the case went to the Court of Chancery. A particular difficulty was caused by the two nuns, who appeared in court in full convent dress and claimed that they had not seen a signature on the paper they had signed years earlier, and that they had believed the paper gave them permission to stay at Nanteos till the end of the war. Their confusion was hardly surprising in the circumstances.

For his own good reasons the judge found the will valid. The personalty was valued at £72,000, which took no account of death duties owing. But another judgment was required to determine the meaning of the codicils. Effectively this gave preference to Mrs Mirylees over the Pryse cousins, and with probate granted in July 1954, her family were able to move into the mansion the following year and assume ownership of the estate. The most important single contribution they made was to gain a considerable grant for the repair of the mansion roof in 1958, without which the house would eventually have become uninhabitable.

The Mirylees family would open the house to visitors during the summer for one day a week, and I have already described a visit there in 1964. However, the Mirylees family eventually realised that Nanteos and its remaining two thousand acres of land were not sustainable and, in 1969 for the first time in its history, Nanteos mansion with its remaining lands were put on the market. The mansion, with a few acres attached, was bought by Geoffrey and Rose Bliss, while most of the farms were purchased by tenants. The library was bought by Richard Booth, the self-proclaimed king of Hay-on-Wye and re-creator of Hay as a Book Town. The family portraits, alas, had long been sold after inferior copies had been made of a few. Mr Bliss found to his disappointment that the fine stone horse and eagles which surmounted the neo-classical gateway to the stableyard had disappeared. There was an ugly Aberystwyth tradition that he had ripped out the Nanteos fireplaces and sold them; this was not true. The Bliss family kept the house dry and largely unspoilt, though they did rent out the second-floor servants' quarters to students from town. At this time too the dried-up lake was cleaned and filled.

Following the resale of the mansion in 1983 by Mr Bliss,

the house went through a wretched period, and by 1989 it was in poor condition. When I asked for permission to visit Nanteos in 1990, I was referred to an address on an industrial estate at Bermondsey, London, and it seemed that the end must be nigh! I was quite wrong. Nanteos had been bought by Mr Gary Hesp, owner of Unistat, wholesalers of stationery, because he and his Herefordshire family had fallen in love with the house and its setting. Mr Hesp had installed a caretaker and begun the process of drying the place out and buying back some of the kitchen equipment. Eventually it was fit to become a guest house with restaurant, though there was a running difficulty with retaining chefs. However, at a date I have yet to discover, the house was bought by Mr Timothy Gwyn-Jones, a developer who was already involved in the restoration of Trawsgoed mansion a few miles away. He eventually had to give up these demanding schemes, and in 2004 sold Nanteos to Mr and Mrs Shane Lipscombe.

This change of ownership meant that the resources necessary to put Nanteos back on a firm footing were available. Years of serious investment have recreated the mansion as a successful five-star country house hotel from 2012. Inevitably this involved changes, most of them invisible to the ordinary visitor. The most obvious alterations, to one who remembers the house over a long period, are that the fine entrance hall now has a counter for reception staff and guests, and the old kitchen, while retaining much of its splendid nineteenth-century equipment, is now the hotel breakfast room. The library is now the main bar. The four vast original main bedrooms have been altered to form suites. But much remains more or less unaltered, especially the inner lobby, the magnificent staircase, the splendid long gallery, the wonderful mirrors and plasterwork in what was the Music Room. The old drawing room retain much of its charm. The cellar is normally closed.

Outside, the only land owned by Nanteos to the immediate south of the mansion is a rather narrow band of grass with parking facilities, but the splendid view across the Paith valley hasn't altered much in decades. To the west, the ornamental lake is now an attractive refuge for otters rather than the place of persecution and death it once was in the days of hunting. Woodland stretches from the west round the northern slope above the mansion. To the east lies the large walled garden, only the nearer half of which is owned by the hotel. Attached to the house are the stables and coachhouse, where restoration has begun but awaits completion at the time of writing (2024). Man's works are not everlasting, but Nanteos mansion looks safe in its present ownership.

9

Nanteos Mansion

THE PRESENT GEORGIAN mansion of Nanteos is of course not the original Neuadd Lawdden house. That would have been a timber building designed as a hall with a central fireplace, with rooms added at one or both ends. This was replaced by a stone building, probably in the seventeenth century thanks to an influx of income from the lead mines, and so possibly commissioned by Cornelius le Brun who had married the Jones heiress in mid-century. The cellars and parts of the walls of that house were perhaps incorporated into the main body of the present mansion, commenced in 1739 on the initiative of Thomas Powell, using his wife's money. This, with later additions, is still the house that now looks south across the Paith valley.

Nanteos house was examined and professionally described by Tony Parkinson in chapter 7 of *Nanteos: a Welsh House and its Families*, and some of what follows is a précis of his admirable work, gratefully used. His diagrams show that the exterior west wall, the interior walls of the main hall and the back wall of the kitchen date from about 1730 (though I venture to suggest they may be earlier). The south and east exterior walls are of the years 1739–59, while the main Dining Room was added about 1848–50. Other interior walls are a mélange from the different periods.

Let's return to the front of the house and consider it more closely. The prospect is of seven window-bays: two pairs flank the central, rather cramped trio, which contain the main door. The house is three storeys high, though there is a fourth low attic storey under the original hipped roof, not visible from ground level. A stone rather obscurely placed to the right of the portico bears a badly worn and now illegible inscription dating the building to 1739, denoting its beginning rather than its completion. That the work took many years is suggested by the surviving downpipes draining rainwater from the roof; they are dated 1757.

In accordance with Palladian practice the windows diminish in height as the eye passes upwards to the balustrade around the roof. By way of contrast the three first-floor windows in the central bay are round-topped, not the usual rectangular form, and above them again are three unusual round windows. The walls are of local stone – Aberystwyth grits – like that visible in the best early houses in Aberystwyth, though the actual quarry is unknown. Although dark, the stone's colouring at its best is sufficiently variegated as not to be boring. However, the walls were originally covered with ashlar, now removed save in the front triple-bay, where it was renewed about 1846–8 and the pillared portico provided, all done by Edward Haycock of Shrewsbury. He may also have designed the classical frontage to the stable courtyard.

Hayward was not the only architect involved with Nanteos. About 1814 John Nash was called on to produce designs for improving the west side of the house, for a new lodge and other buildings, none of which seem ever to have happened, though the lovely designs survived. Later W.R. Coultart was called on to design two wings, but only the east one was built, in 1841. It was styled to match the main block. The billiard room was attached to this wing in the 1860s, possible designed by R.K. Penson.

The conversion of the house to a hotel since 2001 inevitably meant changes to the interior, including division of the first-floor bedrooms: it could not have been otherwise. But much remains unchanged, especially on the ground floor and in the basement and the upstairs gallery. The Entrance Hall has had a reception desk installed but is otherwise unaltered. A family funeral hatchment hangs on the wall. This would have been prepared and placed outside above the main entrance when an owner (possibly W.T.R. Powell or his father W.E. Powell) had died, to show that the house was in mourning for a year. It bears the Powells' motto, *Inter Hastas et Hostes*, meaning 'Between the spears and the enemy'. This is intended to suggest that the head of the family should be willing to advance on the enemy in front of his own troops, challenging the enemy to single combat. This should be seen as heraldic braggadocio rather than as commemoration of any ancestral heroic deeds.

Then we reach the inner hall, with fine old flags on the floor and a splendid original staircase of the mid-eighteenth century. Of the ground-floor rooms, the drawing room has been altered in recent decades, still more or less in character with the past, but the former library is now the hotel bar. A photograph of 1967 shows it still with good shelves and leather-bound books, but the volumes were all carried off by Richard Booth of Hay-on-Wye and others after the 1968 sale, and the shelves have vanished. A block of wallpaper bearing a pattern of books is a sole and disappointing reminder of the room's original function.

The old kitchen, now used as a breakfast room, is off the side hall with the bells to summon servants still hanging in a row under the rooms' original names. The kitchen contains some fine coppers recovered from past sales, and some splendid iron fittings (oven range, heating, etc.). One is clearly the product of one of Aberystwyth's nineteenth-century iron foundries, now entirely vanished. The dining room, like the library, was redesigned with plasterwork by Haycock. The extensive cellar is not open to visitors, since the steps are so irregular and frankly dangerous. I would like to think that it was originally dug for the previous house, Neuadd Lawdden. Its present plan is rather confusing: the wine store was Haycock's work.

On the first floor, the Gallery is impressive, again with plasterwork by Haycock. It could well have served the family's womenfolk as a promenading area during the winter, when frequent rain and the all-pervading mud outside would have made outdoor exercise unattractive. The original main bedrooms led off the two ends of the gallery into the four corners of the house, with the exception of the room at the north-west corner. The three main bedrooms all had dressing rooms, but there has been repartitioning to provide six bedrooms for hotel guests. The north-west room had been the squire's study and bolt-hole, where heads of otters and foxes hung. The room was locked after the death of Edward Athelstan Powell, the last squire, in 1930: its subsequent reopening in the 1950s brought forth a foul stench from the ill-cured animal heads.

The major attraction on this floor is the Saloon, often now known as the Music Room. This would have been where George Powell installed his Broadwood piano, but there is no music here at present. The room has a wonderful display of mirrors: their age, provenance and how they were brought to Aberystwyth are matters for conjecture and admiration. The plasterwork on the walls and ceiling is complex and delightful, as well as being another subject for speculation: is it original eighteenth-century work, or is it a good later imitation of an earlier style?

The fireplace is of high-quality marble, with an inset panel illustrating Aesop's fable of the 'Fox and the Stork'. The fox had invited the stork to supper, which was soup on shallow plates which the fox could lap up, but not the stork. So the stork served the fox a meal in a tall, narrow flask which baffled the fox but gave ample depth for the stork's beak. Moral: each to his own, or in Welsh, *pawb at y peth y bo*. For some time now this room has been used for weddings, hence the white chairs. However, one should try to picture it as if George Powell were still playing classical music on his Broadwood upright piano to a few select friends and invited guests.

The rooms on the Nanteos second floor have been completely transformed recently to be used as guest rooms. I was able to visit them some years ago when they were simply empty and dirty; the students who last lodged here decades ago were long departed.

It's almost impossible for visitors to see the roof of the house, since there is no outside vantage point: it simply, like most roofs, has to be taken for granted. Yet a moment's thought shows that this is every house's most essential feature, and maintaining a roof this size calls for care and resources. I have heard it claimed that at some stage the lead was deliberately taken from the roof, but this was never the case, though of course lead roofing can deteriorate and need repair. Without the provision of steel girders in 1958 and further repairs in the 1990s and 2000s, the house would by now have become a wreck in need of demolition. Happily the fabric of the house is in better condition now than it has been for a century and more.

*

Every country mansion had and has an array of outbuildings of every kind, often altered beyond any recognition of their original purposes. The remarkable features of the Nanteos stableyard are the neo-classical entrance, originally surmounted by carved stone figures of a horse and two eagles, and the yard, still wonderfully cobbled with stones from Tan-y-bwlch beach. Beyond the stables is the still-derelict dove-cote dated to 1816. The building between the mansion and the stables is known as the 'dairy building', but is more reliably described as the laundry.

East of the mansion and stables is the walled garden, known to have existed before 1764, but recreated early in the nineteenth century. Looking out from the front of the house entrance, one sees on the slope beyond the Paith stream an eye-catcher folly, sometimes given the unlikely description of 'kennels'.

Down the drive from the house is the small lake, probably a vestige of the original and more ambitious Davenport plan. Further still is the wedding-cake lodge of 1857 designed by R.K. Penson.

The sudden announcement of the March 2025 closure of Nanteos as a guest house/hotel seems to make it likely that the mansion will no longer be accessible to visitors. Sad though this is, at least the house has been saved from the fate of so many Welsh country houses, as depicted by Thomas Lloyd in *The Lost Houses of Wales* (1986). A generation of visitors has been fortunate enough to have seen the house in good condition when not prevented by the Covid pandemic. Despite its mostly undistinguished members, the family played a major part in Cardiganshire's social and political history.

10

The Nanteos Cup

THE STANDARD ACCOUNT of the Nanteos Cup is that given by Dr Juliette Wood in her chapter in the 2001 *Nanteos* volume; her wide-ranging examination of the folklore surrounding the object remains the only standard academic treatment. However, there has been further research since then which needs to be taken into account. There can hardly be an artefact in Wales about which so much has been written as the Nanteos Cup, much of it fanciful and speculative, to put it kindly, and all of it written after 1878, when it seemed (incorrectly) to have been mentioned in print for the first time. George Powell had lent it for an exhibition at St David's College, Lampeter, when it was described in the catalogue simply as 'a healing cup'. Only about 1900 was it reimagined to be not only the chalice used in the Mass at Strata Florida Abbey, but to be the Holy Grail, supposedly the cup used by Jesus at the Last Supper.

A key event in the birth and growth of the Cup's legend occurred in the summer of 1901. The British Chatauquan Society held its annual gathering at Aberystwyth. This was an offshoot of an American self-education movement founded in 1874 at a camp beside Lake Chatauqua in New York State. It was immensely popular for several decades before finally fading away by 1945. In 1901, British Chatauquan members attending their annual conference at Aberystwyth spent an afternoon at Strata Florida and another at Nanteos. The latter is described in detail by the *Welsh Gazette*. The Rev. George Eyre Evans, a well-known Unitarian minister and local historian, was invited to address the meeting.

Evans attributed the Cup, which was on display, to the Cistercian monks at Strata Florida, who he claimed had used it as a chalice on the abbey's altar. From the monks, he asserted, it had passed to the Stedman family who had bought the abbey and its demesne after the Dissolution of 1536–39. From them it had passed to the Powells. He seems to have been careful not to make any extravagant claims for the vessel, and made no reference to any earlier manifestation, though he wrongly said that the Stedmans had been friends of the monks, rather than their successors. He supported the claims made for it as a healing cup, reading several of the testimonials to its value written by those who had borrowed it. Some of these documents survive today.

George Eyre Evans's address was followed by one from 'Mrs Powell'. Was this Mrs Anna Maria Powell, wife of William Beauclerk Powell, or her daughter-in-law Mrs Margaret Powell? It was the older couple (both died in 1911) who probably hosted the occasion, though they may well have called on son Edward and his wife Margaret to deputise for them. But Mrs Anna Powell could have been involved; she had at some state welcomed to Nanteos the Welsh folklorist and eccentric Jonathan Ceredig Davies, who in 1911 published an account of his meeting her at Nanteos, and examining the Cup, at some earlier time.

He refers to it as supposedly having been made from the timber of Christ's cross, which certainly contradicts the equally unlikely story of it, also cited by Davies, as having been used at the Last Supper.

Mrs Powell, according to the newspaper, described 'certain other remarkable incidents connected with the Cup, which she was able to state from her memory of more than thirty years ago'. These incidents are not specified in the report, but she did claim to remember a time when the Cup had been intact, and that since then considerable damage had been done by 'nibbling pilgrims' anxious to retain a souvenir. She also asserted that at some point a band of gold had been fastened on the rim, which had deprived the Cup of its healing properties, which were only restored when the band was removed.

Even more remarkable claims were made on the same occasion by the Rev. J. Agar Beet, well-known in his day (1840–1924) as a prolific Biblical commentator of the Wesleyan branch of Methodism. He referred to the Cup as 'said to have been the Holy Grail itself'. Clearly by 1901 there was already a popular identification of the Cup with the Holy Grail, supposedly the vessel in which Jesus dispenses wine to his disciples at the Last Supper. A still more remarkable history of the Cup was in a booklet published in 1905, *Lost and Found: a Story of the Holy Grail,* written by Ethelwyn M. Amery.

Amery's text makes it clear, though the Chatauquans are not mentioned, that she was at their meeting at Nanteos in 1901, and she attributes to Mrs Powell the whole story as elaborated in her booklet. The Cup, she asserted without any evidence whatsoever, was that used at the Last Supper; it was brought to Britain by Joseph of Arimathea and left at his supposed foundation of Glastonbury Abbey. Thence, at the abbey's dissolution, seven monks escaped to Strata Florida Abbey in west Wales, where they kept it until, the last monk expiring, it was given to the Stedmans, the new owners of the dissolved abbey. From them it was inherited by the Powells of Nanteos.

None of these stories and associated details has any truth, save only for the fact, attested by 1878, that the Cup, like many others, was believed to have healing powers, especially for bleeding. Jesus's disciples were fishermen and other humble members of their society had more to do than worry about keeping souvenirs of Jesus's death. Vessels in poor Palestinian homes would have been of earthenware, not wood. The Nanteos Cup, at the request of its owners, has not been scientifically examined to prove from what wood it is made. It is not made of olive wood, as has been claimed; that is quite clear to any eye which has seen the knotty grain of olive wood. The best guess, made by the late Douglas Hague, is that it may be the British wych elm. There is no evidence whatever that Joseph of Arimathea (a New Testament character who arranged Jesus's burial after the Crucifixion) ever visited Britain. Glastonbury Abbey cannot possibly have been founded in the first century AD – there we no monasteries anywhere before the fourth century. If a vessel reputed to be the Holy Grail had ever been held at Glastonbury, it would have been famous throughout England and beyond as an object of pilgrimage. Glastonbury was dissolved a year later than Strata Florida, so no monk in his right mind would have escaped to Wales. The Cup could not have been used as the Strata Florida communion chalice because the monks would certainly have owned and used communion vessels of silver or silver-plated metal, and in any case if it had been brought to Strata Florida in 1539, the abbey had already been dissolved. The vessel itself is a simple drinking bowl of the late medieval period which was probably found in the abbey ruins and kept originally as a curiosity.

It needs to be added that the whole mythology of the 'Holy Grail' derives from the French Arthurian romances in the twelfth century and their development of the ideal of the ultimate 'Good Knight', heroic, courteous and virginal. Such a man must have for his quest an objective more spiritual, less worldly than a woman, however beautiful. So heroes, with their origin in Welsh legend, Cai and Bedwyr became Sir Kay and Sir Bedevere, and to their ranks are added Peredur, who becomes Perceval and the purely French creations, Lancelot and Galahad. The Grail never existed as a physical object. Nevertheless the concept intrigues those Christians who believe that archaeological and historical research may reveal 'real' artefacts from Biblical times, such as Noah's Ark, supposedly buried in the snows on Mount Ararat, or the Crucifix, once farcically claimed to be hidden in a cave in Pembrokeshire.

The Nanteos Cup may have gained its healing reputation prior to George Powell's ownership; he himself may have been sufficiently intrigued to help promote it as a healing vessel, but the whole later 'Grail' farrago in the Cup's history is a tissue of fantasy and gullibility. Dr Juliette Wood's authoritative chapter, already referred to, examines in scholarly detail the way such legends develop, including discussions of several other vessels for which similar claims have been made. The Cup was kept at Nanteos until 1967, when it was taken away by the daughters of the Mirilees family until eventually deposited at the National Library of Wales, where it is on permanent display, but no longer available for healing purposes.

Note: *The Nanteos Grail*

At a late stage I had to revise this chapter when I encountered a new publication, *The Nanteos Grail: The Evolution of a Holy Relic*, by John Matthews, Ian Pegler and Fred Stedman-Jones (Amberley Press, 2022). This book develops its theme in exhaustive – and exhausting – detail, but with one notable omission. There is no mention of Dr Juliette Wood's authoritative work on the Nanteos Cup, nor for that matter of *Nanteos: A Welsh House and its Families* (2001). The authors make a considerable effort to disinfect the idea that the Nanteos Cup had its origin in the time and place of Jesus's ministry and crucifixion. Yet they succeed in surrounding it with an air of mysterious sanctity; witness statements like 'its possible connection to the story of the Grail', 'the Cup's supposed journey from the Holy Land to Strata Florida', and 'the Nanteos Cup remains a mystery' (all on page 8).

The volume has many more such statements, including the suggestion that because Cadell ap Gruffudd (brother of the Lord Rhys, the twelfth-century ruler of Deheubarth) became a monk at Strata Florida and is known to have made a pilgrimage to the Holy Land, therefore, 'Of all the possible origins for the seed from which the story of the Nanteos Cup grew, this seems the most likely.' This is an apparently subtle sentence; it makes no claim for Cadell as actual owner of a cup which in truth could not have existed in the twelfth century. Instead he could be 'the seed from which the story... grew' – an unprovable yet un*dis*provable claim. It seems to me rather more reasonable to explain the acceptance of belief in the Cup's healing qualities because of its possible association with Strata Florida's monastic past, and to leave it at that.

Despite my sceptical attitude, I am impressed by the detailed research offered into the recent history of the Cup, especially the authors' discovery of an earlier reference to it (as a healing cup, with no Grail reference) in print in Welsh in 1828, of which I had not previously been aware. This certainly predates the 1878 Lampeter exhibition of the Cup by fifty years. But even to dream of it as being anything more than the wreck of a medieval mazer drinking bowl, used in modern times as a healing cup, requires evidence. *The Nanteos Grail* offers none which would satisfy a serious historian.

Sources for Chapter 10

Ethelwyn M. Amery, *Sought and Found: A Story of the Holy Grail* (1905), rpr. (Aberystwyth: William Jones, 1910).

'Catalogue of the Local Museum Exhibited in the Hall of St David's College, 1878', *Archaeologia Cambrensis*, 10 (1879), 4th ser., p.66.

'Report of the Lampeter Meeting', *Archaeologia Cambrensis*, 9 (1878), 4th ser., pp.337–39.

'Archaeological Notes and Queries: The Cup at Nanteos, Cardiganshire', *Archaeologia Cambrensis*, 5 (1888), 5th ser., pp.170–71.

National Library of Wales, Manuscript Material, NLW 3297B, n.d., 3 paper leaves written in a modern hand, 'Account of Cup coming from Glastonbury to Strata Florida during the time of Abbot Whiting', NLW ex 720.

Douglas Hague, 'Report on Nanteos Cup, 16/3/85', *Handlist of material in the National Library of Wales, Aberystwyth*, Vol. 3, p.60.

Douglas B. Hague, 'An Object of Romantic History', *Cambrian News*, 13 May 1988.

NLW Powell family correspondence, Handlist, Vol. 3, No. 4624–4996.

Juliette Wood, 'Nibbling Pilgrims and the Nanteos Cup: A Cardiganshire Legend' in *Nanteos: A Welsh House and its Families*, edited by Gerald Morgan, Gomer Press, Llandysul, Ceredigion, 2001, ISBN 1-85902-802-0.

In 1965 Gerald Morgan published his first book, and now, sixty years and twenty-five volumes later, comes what might be his last book – but who knows? He doesn't. He has written mainly about Wales, the Welsh language and Ceredigion, while teaching in schools in Flintshire, Ceredigion and Anglesey, and at the University College of Wales, Aberystwyth. He and Enid have celebrated sixty years of marriage, and they have three sons, six grandsons and one great-grandson.

Also by the author:

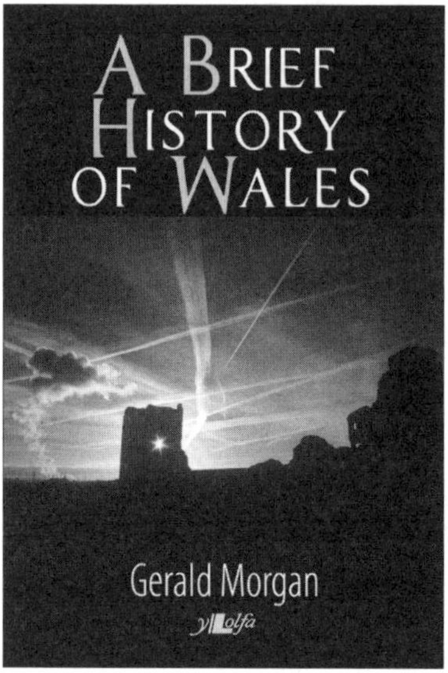

£4.99

£7.99

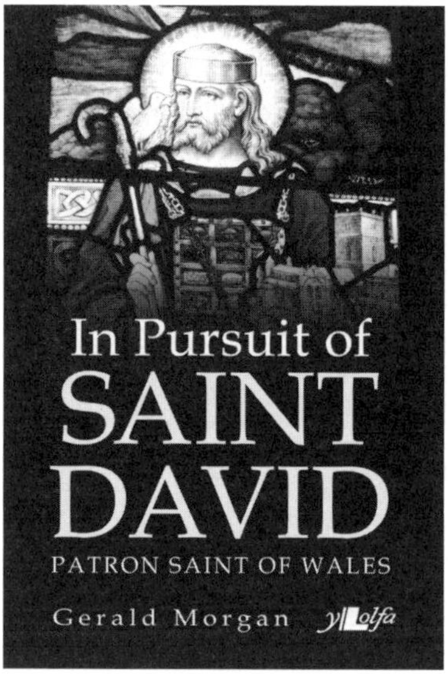

£6.99

£4.95

Also from Y Lolfa:

£8.99